THE SOCIAL SOURCES
OF CHURCH UNITY

ROBERT LEE

THE SOCIAL SOURCES
OF CHURCH UNITY

An Interpretation of Unitive Movements
in American Protestantism

ABINGDON PRESS

NEW YORK • NASHVILLE

THE SOCIAL SOURCES OF CHURCH UNITY

Copyright © 1960 by Abingdon Press

Library of Congress Catalog Card Number: 60-9199

SET UP, PRINTED, AND BOUND BY THE
PARTHENON PRESS, AT NASHVILLE,
TENNESSEE, UNITED STATES OF AMERICA

TO
May, Mellanie, and Marcus

PREFACE

This essay confronts a double neglect: first, the neglect by students of the movement toward Christian unity to discuss social and cultural factors; and secondly, the neglect to treat the positive contribution of social factors in the rise of the church unity movement. In the main attention of previous studies centers on the divisive influence of social forces. Our research seeks to re-apply the insight of H. Richard Niebuhr's *Social Sources of Denominationalism*. While Niebuhr's influential volume interprets church disunity, the focus of the present study is on church unity.

A few guiding remarks are necessary in this preface: The term "church unity" is used as a generic expression. This should not confuse the more seasoned students who prefer to distinguish between "Christian unity" and "church union"— the former referring to the community of thought, feeling, and ethical ideals which provide the basis for fellowship among diverse groups; whereas, the latter suggests institutional forms and visible expressions of unity. We employ the term "church unity" instead of "church union" because the latter phrase is sometimes mistakenly identified solely with *organic union,* which is but one of the many institutional manifestations of unity considered in these pages.

This book consists of three parts. Part I, "The Emerging Unity of American Society," approaches the problem at one level and sketches the background against which later chapters may be viewed. The first two chapters in Part I seek to document the emerging unity of American culture. Readers who do

7

not wish to follow the argument may turn directly to Part II.

Part II, "The Signs of Church Unity," is the heart of the study. Chapters III through VII interpret successively the organizational forms of church unity. These chapters document the development of the various forms of unity and then analyze their social sources.

Part III evaluates the thesis in the light of movements which *appear* to contradict the main interpretation. It presents a succinct report on such movements as denominationalism, sectarianism, fundamentalism, and the Southern Baptist Convention—indicating whether they constitute legitimate countervailing factors. This discussion is followed by a brief summation, which also raises further questions for study.

There is one final point to underscore. Crucial as it is, the theological imperative for Christian unity, treated elsewhere in many treatises, is not dealt with in this volume, whose primary purpose is analysis of the social dimension. By no means does this intend to deny or underrate theological concerns. While our study of social sources may serve as a corrective, it is not a substitute for theological treatment of ecumenicity.

This study should be thought of as exploratory and diagnostic rather than prescriptive. Doubtless, some students of ecumenicity will regard this book as having overstressed the role of social factors; others will wish that the findings be pressed with more vigor. As the case may be, the situation bespeaks both the risk and excitement of scholarship—an adventure, sometimes painful but always pregnant with joy and potentialities for creative growth and discovery.

Countless friends have shared in this adventure. Those I have prevailed upon are too numerous to mention. For critical comments and insights I am indebted to Henry P. Van Dusen, Samuel McCrea Cavert, Alfred S. Kramer, and Robert W. Lynn. A special word of appreciation is due to Robert T. Handy, John C. Bennett, and Charles Y. Glock.

ROBERT LEE

CONTENTS

PART TWO

THE SIGNS OF CHURCH UNITY

Contents

LIST OF TABLES

"Nothing is more mysterious in our human history than the great turnings of the tide in man's striving. We explain them in terms of reaction. . . . We refer the great turnings of history to the mystery of providence, but in the end, we are left facing the sheer givenness of the fact."

Bishop Angus Dun

Prospecting for a United Church (New York: Harper & Brothers, 1948), p. 19.

INTRODUCTION

An unparalleled movement toward church unity in American Protestantism has developed in recent decades. Indeed, friends and foes alike hail this "great new fact of our day" as a potent force of contemporary Protestantism.

Henry P. Van Dusen frequently prophesies that when future church historians chronicle the events of Protestantism in the twentieth century, they will undoubtedly seize upon the ecumenical movement as the single most significant characteristic.

To a degree hitherto unknown, the spirit of co-operation and unity prevails. Documentation of this claim must wait for later attention; but for the moment we must merely stress the fact that a changed religious climate now largely exists.[1]

American church life traditionally has been noted for its religious diversity, for its many and varied religious groups. The bulk of American Protestants today share a different posture. They are astir with the desire to co-operate and unite. An earlier stance, "We ought to do those things together which we cannot do separately," is giving way to the question, "What can't be done better together than separately?" Today religious disunity can no longer be accepted with an

[1] According to Geoffrey Fisher, Archbishop of Canterbury, "Fifty years ago, each side accused the other of some kind of heresy; now the different denominations could meet to compare their treasures instead of their animosities. . . . They are honestly and scientifically trying to clear the ground for the unity of the Church." *Ecumenical Press Service* (November 16, 1956).

easy conscience but is condemned as sinful and scandalous. The problem of this inquiry can be framed simply by this question: What accounts for the surge in the church unity movement in American Protestantism? More specifically, what is the role of social factors in the patterns of emerging church unity?

Excellent grounds exist for the view that social factors play a *negative role* and are responsible for the *disunity* of American Protestantism. For it is well documented that social differences find their counterpart in religious differences.[2] H. Richard Niebuhr's influential study of the role of social factors in creating disunity is a solid source for this view.[3] Niebuhr cogently argues that religious diversity reflects the divisions in American society. Religious proliferation represents not so much theological differences as it does the "accommodation of Christianity to the caste system of human society. . . . The division of the churches closely follows the division of men into the castes of national, racial, and economic groups."[4] At the time Niebuhr's interpretation was a new venture which served to counteract the extreme forms of doctrinal and theological explanations of denominational history. Niebuhr quite rightly scored his point that these explanations are to a large extent mere ration-

[2] Cf. J. Milton Yinger, *Religion, Society and the Individual: An Introduction to the Sociology of Religion* (New York: The Macmillan Company, 1957); Liston Pope, *Millhands and Preachers* (New Haven, Conn.: Yale University Press, 1942); and Elizabeth K. Nottingham, *Religion and Society* (New York: Doubleday and Company, 1954). For example J. Milton Yinger writes: "It is well known that in socially differentiated societies, the various secular groups tend to exhibit differences in doctrine, worship, and religious group structure. This is perhaps the most thoroughly explored area in the field of the sociology of religion. . . . The famous distinction between church and sect, developed by Troeltsch and Weber, is based largely on observation of this fact." "The Present Status of the Sociology of Religion," *The Journal of Religion*, XXXI (July, 1951), 198.

[3] *The Social Sources of Denominationalism* (New York: Henry Holt and Company, 1929). Reprinted by the Shoe String Press, 1954, and by Meridian Books, Living Age Books, 1957. Niebuhr's book has become a *sine qua non* for students of the sociology of the American church.

[4] *Ibid.*, p. 6.

alizations of divisions, which owe their roots to social sources. The essential soundness of Niebuhr's book in theory and application has been widely upheld; his work has become an indispensable part of the storehouse of knowledge in the sociology of religion. Yet we must remember that his analysis of the impact of class, race, sectionalism, and nationalism on church division was published in 1929. No one can deny that these same social factors have since undergone considerable change and erosion.

If we accept Niebuhr's pioneer work as basically sound, and if we apply the analysis of social sources to the current scene, then it seems plausible that current patterns of church unity reflect a unity that has developed in American culture during the intervening years. If, as Niebuhr claims, one cannot understand denominationalism in America solely on doctrinal grounds, but must examine its interplay with social factors, then it would appear necessary to examine the drives toward unity not solely on doctrinal grounds, but also to consider social pressures. If the social factors are responsible for the proliferation of religious groups to a much larger degree than was commonly recognized thirty years ago, then very likely the present-day surge in the movement for church unity is based much more on social factors than is currently acknowledged.

Many studies have examined the correlation between the pluralism of our society and the diversity of our religious behavior; little attention has been given to the reverse proposition —that religious unity might have its counterpart in social unity.

Our thesis is that the increase in church unity springs in considerable measure from the pressures of a growing cultural unity within America society.[5] Social factors, which once pri-

---

[5] Although our study is confined to the American setting, this thesis doubtless has implications for the world-wide ecumenical movement. The "younger churches" of Asia and Africa particularly share in the growing sense of national identity and dignity that mark these independent nations. These churches, which have made such significant contributions to the world-wide movement, must also relate themselves as minority groups to other religions and to governments which are secular and frequently hostile.

marily contributed to the proliferation of religious groups, have been transformed so as to encourage church unity, rather than divisiveness in contemporary American Protestantism. The reduction of religious differentiation stems partially from the erosion of social differences.

The "social sources" which once served as a centrifugal force now tend to function as a centripetal force. At any rate these social factors, in their relation to church unity, have undergone profound changes in a dynamic society. No longer do they represent the same kind of barriers to church unity. In short ecumenicity on the American scene is favored by the increased cultural unity of American society.

Our study will focus attention on the socio-cultural factors in the development of church unity. Concentration on the contribution of these factors is dictated primarily by two challenges. The first is the scarcity of literature and the absence of research on this problem. Little searching study has been directed at the social aspects of ecumenicity. Still less has focused on the positive role of social factors.

The second challenge springs from a growing dissatisfaction with interpretations which point the finger of blame at the so-called "nontheological" or social factors for the church disunity that still exists. In their published documents and "working papers" theologians and ecumenical leaders almost invariably seize upon the negative influences of social and cultural factors.[6] Such interpretations invite review, for they stigmatize

---

Our study is confined to Protestant groups but certainly bears some relevance for the Orthodox and Jewish faiths in America. Marshall Sklare notes that some students of Jewish life confess that growing cultural homogeneity offers the possibility for the emergence of a distinctive "American Judaism" to replace the traditional groupings of Orthodoxy, Conservatism, and Reform. Cf. *Conservative Judaism* (Glencoe, Ill.: The Free Press, 1955), p. 252. The president of the American Jewish Historical Society, Jacob R. Marcus, was even more direct in predicting that American Judaism would be united within the next fifty years in a fusion of the present branches. Cf. *New York Times,* March 29, 1958.

[6] Cf. Winfred E. Garrison, "Social and Cultural Factors in Our Divisions," *Ecumenical Review* (October, 1952), pp. 43-51; H. Paul Douglass, "Cultural Differences and Recent Religious Divisions," *Christendom* (Winter, 1954), pp. 89-

social processes and presuppose a rather static view of society. Once the thesis is established, it should serve to illumine various facets of the movement for church unity in the United States. Social factors should be discernible in the efforts of the religious community to find and develop institutions which are appropriate instruments for the new cultural situation. The reduction of social differences at various levels of ecumenicity should be subject to analysis. The impact of social factors in organic mergers and reunions, in the conciliar movement, in local community-centered churches, and in the practice of comity are appropriate areas of study. Decline in nationality, immigrant, and ethnic churches, and the evolution of sectarian groups provide still more data for examination.

Before treating extensively the various signs and institutions of the church unity movement, we shall devote the next two chapters to exploring the important problem of the emerging unity of American society. We shall then return in succeeding chapters to the impact which the cultural unity has upon church unity.

105; C. H. Dodd, G. R. Cragg, Jacques Ellul, *Social and Cultural Factors in Church Divisions* (New York: World Council of Churches, 1952); H. Obendiek, *The Social and Cultural Factors in Church Division* (London: Student Christian Movement Press, 1953); Daniel Jenkins, "The Ecumenical Movement and Its Non-Theological Factors," *Ecumenical Review* (July, 1951); E. T. Clark, "Non-Theological Factors in Religious Diversity," *Ecumenical Review* (July, 1951).

Note the stress on *diversity* and *division* attributed to social factors in nearly all these writings. One exception is: Willard Sperry, "The Non-Theological Factors in the Making and Unmaking of Church Union" (Geneva: Faith and Order Paper 84, 1937).

PART ONE

THE EMERGING UNITY OF AMERICAN SOCIETY

1. Reduction of Social Differences

I. INTRODUCTION

During the early days of World War II the historian Charles A. Beard announced that if the nation were attacked he would not stir, that even if his state of Connecticut were invaded he would remain calm, but if the enemy approached the town of New Milford he would leap to arms! Such localism is, indeed, rare today. The walls of provincialism and isolationalism have largely crumbled as allegiance to national community consciousness mounts. Many signs of an emerging cultural unity suggest that the idea rests upon firmer foundations than that of poetic imagination. Yet it is a moot point, and many thoughtful observers remain unimpressed.[1]

At first glance, documentation of the emergence of unity as a social pattern in American culture seems well-nigh futile. For observers have repeatedly pointed to the dominance of pluralism and diversity in American society. Less attention is given to its unity and integration.[2]

[1] Cf. George Boas, "Cultural Diversity Within the United States," *The Old and the New World* (Paris: UNESCO, 1956), pp. 269-71.

[2] A notable exception is the sociologist, Robert C. Angell, whose several publications have this theme as their concern. Cf. *The Integration of American Society* (New York: McGraw-Hill Book Company, 1941); A more recent work restates and builds upon the earlier one. Cf. *Free Society and Moral Crisis* (Ann Arbor; University of Michigan Press, 1958). Other signs of increasing concern are Robin M. Williams, *American Society* (New York: Alfred A. Knopf, Inc., 1951); and Arthur J. Vidich and Joseph Bensman, *Small Town in Mass Society* (Princeton: Princeton University Press, 1958); and Will Herberg, *Protestant, Catholic, and Jew* (Garden City, N. Y., Doubleday & Company, 1955). A recent unpublished doctoral dissertation in sociology fastens attention on statistical

21

The reason attention centers on cultural pluralism is not difficult to discern. Pluralism was dramatically evident in the social and historical conditions of nineteenth-century America—the waves of immigrant groups bringing their peculiar traits and contributions to these shores, the fluidity of a developing society with its open frontier, new industries, and new inventions. It is partly due to the traditional stress on such values as individualism, freedom, and competition in the market place of commerce and intellect. In the social sciences, an earlier "social problems approach" centered attention on social pathologies (such as crime, divorce, slums, and race) as single, self-contained units.

Our thesis of emerging cultural unity does not necessarily deny, although it may qualify, the pluralistic view of American society. We are not seeking to advance a monistic interpretation of culture. Nor is the idea of growing national unity predicated on a plea for undifferentiated unity. "Only where there is first differentiation," declares Robin Williams, "can there be integration . . . societies are not integrated by being internally undifferentiated." [3] Unity may also encompass diversity. Indeed, in a recent work, Horace Kallen, an ardent proponent of cultural pluralism, accentuates the need for achieving a high quality of national unity, and sets pluralism within the framework of the "American idea." [4]

---

evidences of uniformity. Cf. E. L. Malone, "The Phenomenon of Increasing Uniformity in Unrelated Areas of the United States" (Columbia University, 1957). Malone draws his study to this conclusion: "In four widely separated areas of the United States, selected as typifying four dissimilar patterns of industrial operations . . . there have existed definite trends toward increasing uniformity. These trends toward homogeneity exist not only in each division of industrial endeavor —agricultural pursuits, professional service, domestic and personal service, trade and transportation, manufacturing and mechanical pursuits, mining and quarrying, but also in each phase of the sociological fields we investigated—urbanization, native-born migrants, per cent Negro population, median age of the population, per cent females married, differential fertility, educational costs, and per capita income." For each of these industrial and sociological patterns, the author presents quantitative data showing a *reduction of disparities* and greater approximation to a national average.

[3] *Op. cit.,* p. 515.

[4] *Cultural Pluralism and the American Idea* (Philadelphia: University of Pennsylvania Press, 1956), p. 113. Kallen wrote a series of provocative articles

22

As a broad, impressionistic generalization, the idea of cultural unity has been forcefully stated by some recent observers as a definite mark of contemporary American life. Thus William S. White, after traveling some 18,000 miles during the 1956 national political campaign (a period at least potentially full of national discord), concludes that he has found a "consensus American," a *homo Americanus*. Political analyst White wrote:

It is an experience of bittersweet quality to feel able to report (but also to be compelled to report) that homo Americanus is now an exact as well as a mere sociological term. The kind of sectional divisions that were arrestingly sharp as recently as fifteen years ago, and vestigially evident as recently as four years ago—these now are all but gone.

There is no longer any South of the kind that was so real only yesterday. . . .

It is not merely in the political sense that the South is no longer solid; it is broken up and assimilated in every sense into a national stream. . . .

Consensus American is now equally at home in Houston and in Hartford.[5]

Somewhat similar conclusions were reached in a more serious work by the historian Henry Steele Commager, who observes that Americans tended more and more to "conform to a type":

in *The Nation* forty years ago in which he combatted the "melting pot" notion as being antidemocratic in a multiculture America. He insisted upon the recognition of the integrity of transmitted cultures from the old world and the right of ethnic diversity, while resisting the idea of being molded into a single form of American culture.

It still remains true, however, that scholarly attention is often diverted from cultural unity (or at least indifferent to it). Commented one historian of American thought: "So much has been written in recent years about the disparate quality of American society, about its conflicting elements and unassimilated groups, that we sometimes forget that we are really a remarkably homogeneous people. . . . No country has ever before taken so many different peoples, speaking so many different languages, and in so short a time assimilated them into one nation with a common tongue . . . and outlook. We have become a people fundamentally unified." Cf. Louis B. Wright, *Culture on the Moving Frontier* (Bloomington, Ind.: Indiana University Press, 1955), p. i.

[5] " 'Consensus American'—A Portrait," *The New York Times Magazine* (November 25, 1956), p. 14.

Certainly the American people of 1950 seemed more standardized than those of 1850. Invention and technology has changed an economy of scarcity to an economy of abundance. . . . Easier communication, urbanization, and the mobility of population combined with a hundred agencies such as the press, the radio and the motion pictures to produce a greater uniformity of character and habit. . . . The advent of America to world power and two world wars encouraged the abandonment of isolation, and the new internationalism made itself felt in the realm of ideas and of social practice, which became increasingly cosmopolitan.

The rich, the middle classes, and the poor came closer to living alike, dressing alike, eating the same food, enjoying the same entertainments, sharing the same advantages than at any time since the Civil War.[6]

Despite these findings by two students of the American scene— one a perceptive journalist, the other a competent scholar—our study cannot rest content with their generalizations. Part I seeks to analyze concretely and critically the indices of an emerging cultural unity.

This unity may be discovered in the manifestations of *consensus;*[7] in the common sharing, which cuts across the potentially divisive social differences of American life. Cultural unity implies increased awareness of a common frame of reference in which people tend to see things from a similar perspective. Hence an important source of emerging cultural unity flows from the reduction of social differences. Our operating hypothesis is that the integration of American society springs largely from these three trends:

1. Social changes which have transpired in such areas as race, class, sectionalism, and nationalism.

2. The emergence of new social patterns, such as mass communications and the "organizational revolution."

---

[6] *The American Mind* (New Haven: Yale University Press, 1950), pp. 406-8.
[7] Other terms used interchangeably are "integration," "cohesiveness," "similarity," and "uniformity." Although we will note that some observers use the terms "conformity" and "homogeneity," we will generally avoid such terms because of their confusing connotations.

3. The persistence of previously existing patterns, such as common value themes and national observances.

What, then, are the signs of growing integration of American society? No single clue is sufficient to demonstrate the emerging cultural unity; its makeup is varied and complex. We must look to the cumulative impact of the evidence as marshalled from many sources. Therefore, we intend to draw on a diverse body of literature, citing both intuitive and qualitative as well as objective and quantitative data. For purposes of analysis, our discussion may be considered under two headings: (1) the reduction of social differences, and (2) the signs of growing cultural unity.[8]

II. AREAS OF DYNAMIC SOCIAL CHANGE

The analysis of social process, as employed in this chapter, centers on social changes which have occurred in American life. It deals with the shifting patterns of social relationships as manifested in new trends. To say that social change in one institutional sphere has repercussions on other areas is now axiomatic. Thus, advancement in class status will affect racial, sectional, and ethnic changes; that these trends do not stand apart in isolation is well to bear in mind in our treatment of the processes of unity.

We will consider a limited number of areas depicting dynamic social changes. Specifically, our focus is on the four factors—race, class, sectionalism, and nationalism—singled out for analysis by H. Richard Niebuhr as conducive to religious disunity.[9]

[8] This distinction is not meant to be entirely consistent, for some of the data with which we deal may be viewed in either category. It is rather a convenient way of handling the mass of material. For the most part, our level of abstraction will remain fairly simple in the sense of dealing with concrete facts and data, rather than conceptualizing at several steps removed from the data.

[9] Another area which merits treatment is the blurring of the once sharp distinction between rural and urban places, the rise of metropolitan regions and of "megalopolis." Consider the urban impact on one religious group—Disciples of Christ. At the turn of the century, this group was 93 per cent rural; but today the Disciples are over 60 per cent urban. Another fact selected at random is the radical shift in policy adopted at the last meeting of the National Farmers Union, a group traditionally stressing the independent small farm. The conven-

Recall our contention that these factors have been transformed in recent decades, so that their divisive influences are mitigated. Hence we deal with unity which emerges from the *reduction of social differences.*

A. RACE. Common sense observation of contemporary events might well lead one to conclude that racial conflict and inequality provide ample evidence for the disunity of American society. Indeed, the unresolved race problem contains elements which go counter to our thesis of cultural unity. Any objective analysis of the current scene would concede this point. We must confess that churches are still largely divided along racial lines. Yet, when viewed as a social process—particularly since Niebuhr's 1929 social context—what a veritable revolution has taken place in race relations! Obviously not a simple picture, progress is often marred by setbacks, particularly in various pockets of the nation. While the problem remains, its proportions have been recast. Consider these developments:

1. Students of the race problem have generally surmised that since World War II more progress has been achieved than compared with the combined historical period extending from the Civil War to the beginning of World War II.

2. Since 1952 a single case of lynching is recorded, while prior to that an annual crop of lynchings was recorded since the Civil War. There have been substitute forms of intimidation, bombing, and even murder; but employed as an *institutionalized* form of expressing *community* hostility, lynching has virtually disappeared.

3. In practically every sphere of life, minority group participation has increased markedly—especially in the entertainment fields, but also in politics, trade unions, and education. Opportunities for higher education for Negroes jumped 2,500 per cent since 1930. In fact, many more Negroes attend college in

---

tion not only invited, but urged industry to come to rural areas in order to achieve a better balance for farmers, *New York Times* (March 21, 1958). Also cf. Vidich and Bensman, *op. cit.* It is apparent that the social differences, which once grew out of the urban-rural dichotomy, have been considerably reduced.

26

the United States than do British subjects in all British universities in England, Scotland, Wales, and North Ireland (160,000 for U.S. Negroes as compared to 105,461), though the respective population bases are 16,000,000 and 45,000,000.[10]

4. For the first time in eighty-two years, the United States Congress passed civil rights legislation in 1957. Of great significance is the fact that the filibuster was not employed to obstruct civil rights legislation.

5. The Supreme Court decision on school desegregation on May 17, 1954, is hailed by some as equal in significance to the Emancipation Proclamation of 1863.[11]

To be sure, considerable conflict and tension have accompanied these social changes. Yet conflict often provides the milieu from which social change emerges. At hand is also evidence of organized resistance and retrenchment in intergroup relationships in some localities. But the over-all scene is certainly marked by change in the direction of greater equality and wider application of the national policy of insistence upon equal rights, as evidenced by the Supreme Court's reaffirmation of its 1954 decision.

Changes are also noted in the realm of attitudes and beliefs. Surveys of the National Opinion Research Center report major increases in the percentage of whites who are willing to live in mixed communities, travel on public vehicles without separation of races, and accept integrated education. Even Southerners are changing their opinion as rapidly as people in other parts of the nation. In response to the question, "Do you think Negroes are as intelligent as white people?" the answers in 1942 indicated that only 21 per cent of white Southerners answered "yes," but 38 per cent answered in the affirmative in 1956.

Although the center of attention rightly focuses on the plight of America's nearly 16,000,000 Negroes, one should not forget

[10] *Basic Facts and Figures* (Paris: UNESCO, 1952), p. 28. American data are for 1954, and British for 1949-50.
[11] Although many of the ramparts of racism have been assaulted, the writer by no means intends to counsel complacency in citing significant advances. Major setbacks include the Little Rock, Arkansas, school crisis.

that large segments of the Oriental population have been quite undramatically assimilated into the main stream of American life. So marked has been this trend that one sociologist could write a monograph on the "Decline of Chinatowns in the United States." [12] The decentralization of these racial enclaves proceeds at a rapid pace. They are sustained largely by their business and commercial base, which caters to the curiosity of tourists seeking a "bit of Cathay." Many Chinatown shopkeepers, like other merchants, commute to and from the suburbs. The rate of assimilation for Japanese-Americans is even more impressive.[13]

In later chapters we will have occasion to see how race retards or contributes to church unity. Several introductory comments are in order in the present context. Richard Niebuhr surmises, in his *Social Sources of Denominationalism*, that unlike sectional and national sources of church schisms, which give promise of healing, racial schisms are steadily growing more acute and scarcely affect the church union movement." [14] Perhaps still somewhat true, this judgment at least stands in need of qualification.

Here and there, one encounters significant signs indicating that church disunity due to race has given way owing to the erosion of racial differences. In Stockton, California, a Negro, a white, and an Oriental church have merged to form one fellowship.[15] Other instances of the merging of racially dissimilar churches are known. In several cases of internal conflict between first and second—or third—generation Japanese-American churches, the second generation group has chosen the way of assimilation, preferring to sever their relationships with the dwindling "Isseis" than to remain a segregated institution. Now and again, one hears of an Oriental pastor or a Negro minister

[12] Rose Hum Lee, "The Decline of Chinatowns in the United States," *American Journal of Sociology* (March, 1949).
[13] Cf. Robert Lee, "The Acculturation of Chinese-Americans," *Sociology and Social Research*, 36 (May-June, 1952).
[14] *Op. cit.*, p. 259.
[15] Wilbur Choy, "Integration by Merger," *The City Church*, VIII (January-February, 1957), 6-8.

serving an all-white congregation, but this event is newsworthy and remains the exception rather than the rule.[16]

Perhaps the most significant modification of Niebuhr's judgment is the trend toward interracial churches and mixed congregations, particularly outside the South. For these churches reflect a reduction in social differences, which in turn provides the occasion for the reduction of religious schismatic tendencies.

The author of a frequently cited book wrote in 1948 that he could not find "a single 'white' church with an 'open' or mixed membership in an area undergoing transition"; that perhaps less than five per cent of white churches have any Negro members; and that less than one half of 1 per cent of Negro Christians are found in white churches.[17] Yet subsequent studies have spotted and reported upon a whole host of integrated churches *in areas of transition.* S. Gary Oniki has written case studies on some twenty interracial congregations.[18] In 1950, a survey of Presbyterian, U.S.A., churches found 832 "integrated" out of 2,706 reporting churches.[19] A New York City Protestant Council study claims that "about half of the Protestant churches in the four Boroughs have an inter-racial following of some sort." A 1958 study of Congregational-Christian churches in metropolitan areas found that 12 per cent of them include Negro members, and that 49 per cent are willing to accept Negroes as members. Liston Pope makes the over-all statistical estimate that about 10 per cent of the total number of Protestant churches

[16] When Dean Andrew F. Murray of Lincoln University's school of theology announced the closing of the Seminary as of June, 1959, he reported that small enrollments are plaguing all Negro theological institutions. In view of the high level of enrollment elsewhere, one wonders whether Negro seminarians are choosing to attend non-Negro seminaries.

[17] Frank S. Loescher, *The Protestant Church and the Negro* (New York: Association Press, 1948) , p. 79.

[18] "Inter-racial Churches in American Protestantism," *Social Action,* XVI (January 15, 1950) , 4-22.

[19] *Social Progress,* XLVII (January, 1957) . This entire issue reports also on seven case studies of Presbyterian integrated churches in selected sections of the nation. None of these cases was included in the earlier Oniki report.

are interracial, and that this figure is five times as great as that of ten years ago.[20]

In terms of social process, we may lift up three factors:

a) Population mobility has led hundreds of thousands of Negroes from rural areas to cities, both North and South. This broader geographical dispersion of Negroes has resulted in a more uniformly distributed racial composition for the nation as a whole.

b) Social changes of a structural nature are striking at the foundations of segregation. Population mobility, noted above, has an impact on the Negroes' changing class and caste status.[21] Largely a thing of the past is the one-crop cotton, plantation economy as a way of life. Changes in urbanization and industrialization bring new social patterns in their wake.[22] In an urban social context, interpersonal relations are "segmental" and social relations more impersonal; hence an individual is judged not so much by who he is, but by how well he can perform a function. These influences make for growing similarity.

c) Finally, one may expect that schisms of racial churches growing out of vast differences in cultural and class levels will be reduced, if greater employment and educational opportunities, which help to achieve a common cultural level, are available. To some aspects of this problem we turn our attention next.

B. CLASS. Of the various areas of social research that command the interest of American sociologists, class stratification stands near the top. Yet, for the most part, the spate of community studies sheds little light on our problem. Their point

[20] Liston Pope, *The Kingdom Beyond Caste* (New York: Friendship Press, 1957).

[21] For an admirable sociological study of the new middle-class Negro cf. E. Franklin Frazier, *Black Bourgeoise* (Chicago: The Free Press of Glencoe, Ill., 1957).

[22] For example, one cannot overlook or underestimate the political power of the Negro vote in the North, and increasingly in the South. The same goes for the Negroes' economic purchasing power, which is increasingly being recognized by national advertisers.

of departure entails the documentation of the existence of a class system, the number and behavior patterns of various classes, and their interrelations with other items in the community.

By and large, these community studies leave the impression that class lines are solidifying and opportunities for mobility have been seriously curtailed. Such a static picture is inadequate and misleading; it overlooks data on intergenerational mobility in occupations and larger bodies of statistics than those obtainable in a particular community analysis.[23]

Compare the Lynds' pioneer *Middletown* study with their study of Middletown revisited.[24] In the earlier volume, the Lynds suggested a simple twofold class system: "Business Class" and "Working Class." In the second study, however, apart from suggesting a schema of six groups, the Lynds document the rise of a new group of middle-class, white-collar citizens. In microcosm the rise of the middle class of *Middletown in Transition* is the story of America in transition.

The middle class has expanded in fact as well as in the self-identification of the bulk of the American people.[25] Of the

[23] Cf. William Petersen, "Is America Still the Land of Opportunity?" *Commentary* (November, 1953); Natalie Rogoff, *Recent Trends in Occupational Mobility* (Chicago: The Free Press of Glencoe, Ill., 1953); Suzanne Keller, "The Social Origins of Three Generations of American Business Leaders" (unpublished Ph.D. thesis, Columbia University, 1953), Seymour Lipset and Natalie Rogoff, "Class and Opportunity in Europe and the United States," *Commentary* (December, 1954). Cf. especially Gideon Sjoberg, "Are Social Classes in America Becoming More Rigid?" *American Sociological Review*, 16 (December, 1951), 775-83. For a comprehensive survey of the literature on the amount of social mobility cf. Bernard Barber, *Social Stratification* (New York: Harcourt, Brace and Company, 1957), pp. 422-71.

[24] Robert S. Lynd and Helen Merrell Lynd, *Middletown* (New York: Harcourt, Brace and Company, 1929), and *Middletown in Transition* (New York: Harcourt, Brace and Company, 1937).

[25] Joseph A. Kahl, *The American Class Structure* (New York: Rinehart & Company, 1957), pp. 160-71. The startling 1940 Fortune poll reported that 80 per cent of Americans regarded themselves as "middle class." A similar Gallup poll discovered that 87 per cent located themselves in the middle class. However, the respondents only had three alternatives in answering the survey question; the choices were "Upper Class," "Middle Class," and "Lower Class." Subsequent studies which offered more alternatives reveal that between 40 to 50 per cent of Americans locate themselves in the middle class.

many variables which comprise the measurement of class status, we will deal with two for purposes of noting changes. These are occupation and income—or shifts in the source and amount of income.

Table 1 (page 32) indicates the distribution of the working population in the United States by major occupational groups. Note the sharp decline of farm laborers, farm owners, and unskilled workers; the rise of the white-collar occupations and of skilled workers.

TABLE 1

SOCIAL-ECONOMIC DISTRIBUTION OF LABOR
FORCE, MEN AND WOMEN: 1870, 1910, 1950 [26]

Social-Economic Group	Percent of 1870	Labor 1910	Force 1950
Professional Persons	3%	4.4%	8.5%
Proprietors, Managers:			
Farmers	24	16.5	7.3
Others	6	6.5	8.6
Clerks, Salespeople, kindred	4	10.2	18.9
Skilled Workers and Foremen	9	11.7	13.8
Semiskilled Workers	10	14.7	21.7
Unskilled Workers:			
Farm Laborers	29	14.5	4.3
Non-Farm Laborers	9	14.7	8.3
Servant Classes	6	6.8	6.3
Not Reported			2.3
Total 100%		100%	100%

A closer look at the decline of agricultural workers in the labor force is given in Table 2:

[26] *Ibid.*, p. 67. Copyright, © 1957, by Joseph A. Kahl.

TABLE 2

PROPORTION OF THE WORKING POPULATION
OCCUPIED IN AGRICULTURAL PURSUITS[27]

Year	1870	1910	1950
California	21.5%	20.3%	8.2%
Iowa	61.4%	42.9%	28.6%
Pennsylvania	25.9%	11.5%	4.3%
South Carolina	78.7%	70.4%	26.8%

Table 2 reveals that the proportion of agricultural workers has declined markedly in each of four states located in different parts of the nation.

Technological changes, the expansion of the American economy, and changes in the methods of business management have ushered in a large corps of middle-class workers to handle the administrative, office, and paper work—a development sometimes dubbed the "second industrial revolution." White-collar workers increased in numbers from 5,115,000 in 1900 to 21,600,000 in 1950; they constitute 36.6 per cent of the working population in 1950 as compared to 17.6 per cent in 1900.[28] The noted economist Sumner H. Slichter, impressed by the emergence of a middle-class society, cited these facts:

Between 1900 and 1950, the number of engineers increased from 41,000 to 850,000.

The number of common laborers dropped from 8.9 million in 1910 to 5.9 million in 1956, and from one-fourth of the employed persons to one eleventh.[29]

Not only has the composition of the labor force changed with new professions and semiprofessional specialties laboratory

[27] Malone, *op. cit.,* p. 123.
[28] United States Census Bureau, "News Release" (August 31, 1958).
[29] "The Growth of Moderation," *Atlantic Monthly,* 198 (October, 1956), 62. For other statistics cf. C. Wright Mills, *White Collar* (New York: Oxford University Press, 1951), pp. 63-76; and Lewis Corey, "The Middle Class," *Class, Status and Power,* eds. Reinhard Bendix and Seymour M. Lipset (Chicago: The Free Press of Glencoe, Ill., 1953), pp. 371-80.

and x-ray technicians, electronic technicians, and public administration aides—but also the proverbial "income pie" is being sliced in different ways. Changes in the distribution of income may be seen from Table 3.

TABLE 3

DISTRIBUTION OF INCOME, 1929, 1951 [30]

Income	1929	1951
Under $3,000 ....65%		46%
Over $3,000 (to $7,500) 29%		47%
Over $7,500 .... 6%		7%

C. Wright Mills observed that instead of the traditional pyramid with a flat base, today the picture portrays a fat diamond with a bulging middle.[31] What has been dubbed the "fat 50's" reflects higher wages and a more equal distribution of wealth.

The leveling of per-capita income is attested to in Table 4 (page 34), which indicates a steady decrease in the disparities of per capita income in each of four states and in relation to the nation as a whole. Such reduction of per-capita income differences makes for greater cultural similarity.

TABLE 4

PER CENT DIFFERENCE BETWEEN PER-CAPITA
INCOME AND THE PER-CAPITA UNITED STATES INCOME [32]

Year	1929	1940	1950
California 39	40	22
Iowa 20	16	2

[30] Data adapted from figures presented in *Business Week* (Oct., 1952), 28-29. The income for both 1929 and 1951 is in terms of 1951 dollars.

[31] *Ibid.* Also cf. Russell Lynes, *Surfeit of Honey* (New York: Harpers & Brothers, 1957).

[32] Malone, *op. cit.*, p. 108

Year	1929	1949	1950
Pennsylvania	13	9	7
South Carolina	62	50	42
Sum of the Differences	134	115	73

With respect to higher wages, all segments of the population have shared in these gains; but those at the bottom rungs of the economic ladder have gained proportionately more. Taxation has affected those in the top brackets more seriously, while those at the bottom have enjoyed increased living standards. Thus class disparities tend to diminish as income spread has declined markedly.

Slichter provides data which vividly illustrate this point. Between 1935-36 and 1950, the average income among the one fifth of the families at the bottom of the income scale gained 78 per cent in purchasing power, whereas the average income of the 5 per cent at the top of the income scale gained only 17 per cent in purchasing power.[33] This may be partly attributed to the large number of working women—including wives—who "double up" income within families. Lessening of the gap in wages between skilled and professional or technical workers is seen in the fact that one out of five families of skilled craftsmen has an income of more than $7,000 per year. Among technical workers and professional families the proportion is one out of six, and among sales and clerical workers, only one out of seven. These facts lead Slichter to conclude that one out of five skilled craftsmen and their families are able to live better than seven out of ten managers and business owners and their families![34]

Apparently class lines have become blurred and considerable social mobility and fluidity still exists.[35] More and more

[33] Slichter, *op. cit.*, p. 62.
[34] *Ibid.*
[35] Whether it is easier to move into the top socio-economic strata today than formerly is a moot point, which is not germane to our discussion. Studies report ambivalent findings, largely depending upon what indices of mobility are chosen.

people take advantage of education as the vehicle of vertical mobility. Since the 1880's the number of students in schools of higher education has increased about seventeen times in contrast to a population increase of only two-and-a-half times. More Americans now own than rent their homes; the car, washing machine, TV set, and, increasingly, the food freezer are becoming standard equipment in American homes, almost without regard to class status.

More people sharing increasingly in the same goods and services suggests a drastic modification of the picture of class division. The increased numbers in white-collar professions and the minimizing of differences between "working-class" and "middle-class" occupations imply a reduction in social differences due to class—a difference which in the past has kept churches apart. If class differences are modified, then one might expect more fertile ground for the emergence of church unity.

With the shifts in both the source and amount of income, the emergence of a new middle class bears significance for unity. For in large measure, the middle class sets the cultural tone, sustains and perpetuates cultural values, comprises the bulk of the consuming audience for the books and magazines of the mass media, keeps the wheels of organizational life grinding, provides much of the talent and the new recruits for the so-called "serving" professions—education, the ministry, social work. In short, the American middle class constitutes a pivotal and mediating force; it forms the nucleus of the common-core American culture.

C. SECTIONALISM. American historians, geographers, and sociologists have been drawn to the study of sectionalism in such wide currency that it approaches a "school" of thought embraced by its disciples as a fruitful way of interpreting American life and history. The pioneer studies of Frederick Jackson Turner, whose work gave prominence to the idea, and the contributions of Howard Odum and Rupert Vance, and their numerous students, have made sectionalism one of the seminal ideas of the recent past.[36]

Artists, and particularly novelists—William Faulkner, Erskine Caldwell, and John Steinbeck—have discovered in sectional *mores* much ore for their mining. In short, there is considerable fascination for studying the adaptation of people to places and the peculiar folkways, traditions, scenery, climate, and institutions of various parts of the nation.

Our concern in this section is to examine what has happened to sectionalism in thought and practice. If indeed it ever occupied a permanent place in the precincts of scholarship, the concept of sectional autonomy no longer prevails. As a concept, sectionalism has given way to the newer idea of *regionalism*, the former term having a connotation of isolation and cultural insulation, which contemporary events and technological advances have rendered obsolete. Such transition is perhaps best gleaned through the eyes of the perceptive Nobel prize winner, novelist Thomas Mann, who offers this aphorism: "As isolation makes for difference, so difference makes for comparison, comparison gives rise to uneasiness, uneasiness to wonderment, wonderment tends to admiration, and finally admiration turns to a yearning for mutual exchange and unity." [37]

According to Howard Odum the older concept of sectionalism assumes isolated and segregated geographical and cultural units which are self-sufficient entities, whereas the newer idea of regionalism implies a "great national unity in which each region exists solely as a component unit of the whole . . . a unifying

[36] Frederick Jackson Turner, *The Significance of the Frontier in American History* (Proceedings of the State Historical Society of Wisconsin, 1893); Frederick Jackson Turner, *The Significance of Sections in American History* (New York: Henry Holt and Company, 1932); Rupert Vance and Nadia Danilevsky *All These People* (New York: Henry Holt and Company, 1945); Howard W. Odum and Harry E. Moore, *American Regionalism* (New York: Henry Holt and Company, 1938).

[37] Quoted by Howard Odum, "The American Blend: Regional Diversity and National Unity," *The Saturday Review of Literature*, XXXII (August 6, 1949), 92.

function . . . with the integrating power of co-ordinate regions fabricated into a united whole." [38]

Many students of regionalism have rejected Turner's original formulations as having a schismatic and even imperialistic view.[39] One such polemic against sectionalism, waged by the late Louis Wirth, charged it with being a "one factor theory," which furnishes a distorted picture of social reality and overlooks the integrative tendencies taking place on a wider scale. In reply, Howard Odum claims that Wirth's criticisms are directed at the older conception of sectionalism. Odum, however, does agree that Turner's formulation affords "greater difficulties in integrating the whole national organism." The shifting emphasis, from the real or imagined divisiveness of sectionalism to the interrelatedness and unifying idea of regionalism, may itself reflect the reality of sectional changes taking place in American life. This practical point now claims our attention.

With the passing of the frontier—which for most Americans is no longer even a memory—and the rapid industrial and population growth of the West, perhaps the most distinctive region remaining in America today is the South. If the distinction of being the most persistent and self-conscious region belongs to the South, note that pervasive social changes are also quickening her toward greater similarity with the rest of the nation. In a significant issue of the *Virginia Quarterly Review*, three perceptive students of Southern life celebrate the changes with articles bearing these revealing titles, "The Urban Breakthrough in the South," "The Erosion of Sectionalism," and "An Epitaph for Dixie." [40]

[38] Odum and Moore, *op. cit.*, pp. 18, 39, 43.

[39] Cf. Donald Davidson, "Regionalism as Social Science," *Southern Review*, 3 (1937-38), 209-24; and Rupert Vance, "The Regional Concept as a Tool for Social Research," *Regionalism in America*, ed. Merrill Jensen (Madison: University of Wisconsin Press, 1951), pp. 119-40.

[40] Rupert Vance, "The Urban Breakthrough in the South," *Virginia Quarterly Review*, 31 (Spring, 1955); V. O. Key, "The Erosion of Sectionalism," *Virginia Quarterly Review*, 31 (Spring, 1955); and Harry S. Ashmore, "An Epitaph for Dixie," *Virginia Quarterly Review*, 31 (Spring, 1955).

Vance notes that this popular slang expression enjoys wide currency throughout the South: "Cotton's going West, cattle coming East, Negroes going North, Yankees coming South, and money's coming in." It happens to be fairly accurate, and, as Vance maintains, future urbanization will hardly leave a facet of Southern life unchanged.[41]

V. O. Key cautions us to look at the deeper trends rather than the superficial flurries currently marking the Southern scene.[42] Social and economic changes are eroding the foundations of sectional insulation. From 1930 to 1950 the Southern population in cities of 50,000 or more increased at three times the rate of the nation as a whole—resulting in an enlarging urban middle class and a corresponding decrease of agricultural workers. In effect, Key contends, the South is undergoing similar economic reorganization and population relocation experienced by the North and East at the beginning of the twentieth century. Hence Southern sectionalism is a "layer of sentiment and tradition worn thin by the stream of time and events." [43]

Additional social data are noted in Ashmore's wistful piece in which he nostalgically recounts the transformation of the South:

The gasoline engine which powered the auto also powered new tools of mechanized agriculture, reducing the demand for hand labor, which was the base of the sharecropping system. The steady increase of industrial job opportunities began to lessen the bitter economic competition between Negro and whites. . . . The fabulous growth of the cities and the corresponding decline of the rural South, brought a great expansion of the white-collar-middle-class, deeply wounded in the pocketbook by taxes and ready to provide the Republicans a respectable base upon which to erect a second party. The unions followed the factories South. . . . And the great redistribution of population pulled down the proportion of Negroes

[41] Vance, *op. cit.*, pp. 223, 225.
[42] *Op. cit.*, p. 163.
[43] *Ibid.*, p. 164.

to whites to such a degree that the maintenance of legal segregation began to lose its urgency over much of the region.[44]

The above citation offering an admirable summary of social change was written by one who seems resigned to the inevitable fate of the decline and erosion of Southern sectionalism—however shattering and painful that destiny portends.

In pointing to sectional changes in concept and in fact, we have no quarrel with the idea of regionalism. By no means are we prepared to announce an "epitaph" for regionalism. In the main, regionalism is like a spoke in the larger wheel of national unity. Unlike sectionalism, which implies uniqueness and conflict, regionalism is a complementary notion.

Over against our interpretation, some would argue that a unified American culture existed on the frontier, and, therefore, why not an expression of church unity to accompany it? Whoever adopts this view must face the fact that the pioneer characteristics faded fast. In addition recent scholarship shows that more diversity filled the frontier than is commonly assumed. Fluidity was the frontier's most striking feature, as frontiersmen shook loose from the fixity of the past and as different waves of ethnic groups and social classes settled. As Paul W. Gates of Cornell University averred:

> Society on the frontier . . . was more complex, had a wider range of economic well-being than Frederick Jackson Turner thought. The early appearance of farm laborers and tenants, many of whom were never to rise to farm-ownership status, and of great landed estates, whose owners brought wealth with them . . . did not make for a "fundamental unity in its [frontier's] social structure and its democratic ideals." . . . Concepts of the homogeneity of frontier society, similarity of frontier outlook, common addiction to democratic principles, may well be questioned.[45]

[44] *Op. cit.*, pp. 184 ff. Used by permission.
[45] Reprinted with permission of the copyright owners, the Regents of the University of Wisconsin, from Walker D. Wyman and Clifton B. Kroeber, eds., *The Frontier in Perspective*, © 1957, the University of Wisconsin Press.

Indeed, older sectional differences, particularly the frontier society of the West and the slavery-rife culture of the South, have been correlated with religious schisms and the burgeoning of new sectarian groups.[46] Born on the frontier were such groups as the Disciples of Christ and the Cumberland Presbyterian Church. Other groups, notably Methodist, Baptist, and Presbyterian, expanded rapidly with the growing frontier.

Sectional differences have largely eroded under the impact of such factors as common exposure to mass communications, easy accessibility of various transportation media—so that flying by jet from coast to coast becomes a mere matter of hours—the growth of industrialization, the rise of urbanization, and increased personal contact stimulated by population mobility. Moreover, sectional autonomy has increasingly been demolished in the face of common adaptation to an emerging national culture with its nationwide application of moral standards and valuations.

As sectional differences decline one might expect sectional schisms to heal. One might expect to find church unions consummated across sectional lines, reflecting institutional consensus rather than divergence. We shall have occasion to examine cases of such reaction, as well as countervailing instances, in subsequent chapters.

D. NATIONALISM.[47] Perhaps no other area of social life illustrates better the fruitfulness of the analysis of social process than the study of nationality groups. For in studying immigrant, ethnic groups, sociologists have identified the operation

---

[46] Niebuhr, *op. cit.*, pp. 135-200; W. W. Sweet, ed., *Religion on the American Frontier*, 4 vols. (Chicago: University of Chicago Press, 1931, 1936, 1939, 1946) ; and Elizabeth Hooker, *Religion in the Highlands* (New York: Home Missions Council, 1933) .

[47] The use of the term "nationalism" is somewhat infelicitous in view of its political connotations. We are following Niebuhr's use of the term and his application in discussing ethnic and immigrant groups of national origin. Of course, nationality groups are not without their political and cultural significance. For an excellent discussion of the relationship between political, religious, and ethnic bases of nationalism cf. Salo W. Baron, *Modern Nationalism and Religion* (New York: Harper & Brothers, 1947) , pp. 4 ff.

of deep-going sociological processes. These include contact, conflict, accommodation, acculturation, and assimilation—processes which ethnic groups undergo more or less in the course of generations of adaptation to the American scene. For our purposes, a somewhat abridged version of this development may be depicted.

According to this familiar schema, the initial contact between people of varying ethnic traditions and cultures issues in competition and conflict, until the groups arrive at a *modus vivendi:* usually the subordinate group gives way to the superordinate one. Hence accommodation or a form of adjustment is achieved in their intergroup relationships. The shaping of new attitudes and increased positive contacts and adjustment in the way of life of the new group (e.g., educational and economic opportunities), result in acculturation, or the adoption of cultural forms and values of the dominant cultural group. Further association—including intermarriage—leads to assimilation or complete identification. In the final stage, the ethnic group loses its identity and becomes part of the larger community. According to the classic definition of this final stage by the Chicago socioligists Robert E. Park and Ernest W. Burgess:

> Assimilation is a process of interpenetration and fusion in which persons and groups acquire the memories, sentiments, and attitudes of other persons or groups, and, by sharing their experience and history, are incorporated with them in a common cultural life.[48]

The processes of group interaction, then, typically move from disunity to social unity. Countless immigrant Americans have doubtless conformed to these social processes in their adaptation to American life.

Two students of the American scene have observed the significance of ethnic groups in shaping American culture. Oscar Handlin remarks, "Once I thought to write a history of the

---

[48] *Introduction to the Science of Sociology* (2nd ed.; Chicago: University of Chicago Press, 1924), p. 735.

immigrants in America. Then I discovered that the immigrants *were* American history." [49] And Margaret Mead, in her delightful book, *And Keep Your Powder Dry,* writes that "we are all third generation Americans." [50]

While these two statements smack of exaggeration, in a sense they are symbolically, if not literally, true. Recall that Franklin D. Roosevelt once addressed the D.A.R. "Fellow immigrants." The story of immigration may well start from the very beginning of the nation's history. However tenacious our ethnic ties, over the course of several generations, they tend to erode and flow into the mainstream of American culture. Even the newcomer seeks to adopt the behavior patterns of the third generation and tries to shed or conceal the badges of his own traditions. In this sense, he is also third generation.

For our purposes of noting the growing trend toward church unity, the saga of mass migrations in the nineteenth century is highly significant. During the last century European immigrants descended in successive waves. Beginning about 1830, the first wave reached its highpoint in 1854 when 400,000 came to the New World. Another wave, from about 1865 to 1900 overwhelmed the earlier one in numbers, with 800,000 arriving in the year 1882. The third tide of immigration became a veritable flood, lasting until World War I; in each of three years the newcomers reached the million mark, with the top figure being 1,250,000 in 1907. One can well imagine the multiplicity of tongues and traditions which were transplanted by the "Atlantic migration," and how each group would want to sing praises and worship in its own accustomed manner. To this story is added a climax, if not, indeed, a finale. As Will Herberg put it:

This "epic story of the great migrations that made the American people" came to an end substantially with World War I and with

[49] *The Uprooted; the Epic Story of the Great Migrations That Made the American People* (Boston: Little, Brown & Company, 1951), p. 3.
[50] New York: William Morrow & Company, 1942, pp. 27-53.

43

the restrictive legislation of the 1920s. By that time 35,000,000 Europeans had reached these shores: 4,500,000 from Ireland, 4,000,000 from Great Britain, 6,000,000 from central Europe, 2,000,000 from the Scandinavian lands, 5,000,000 from Italy, 8,000,000 from eastern Europe, and 3,000,000 from the Balkans. This was America.[51]

Immigration was slowed down to a trickle by the legislation of 1921 and 1924; Southern Europeans and Asiatics were particularly affected. As a result the foreign-born white population which was 14.5 per cent of the total population in 1910, fell to only 7 per cent by 1950. The 1960 figures will doubtless yield a still lower percentage, so that in time the foreign-born element will become negligible. In view of less favorable quotas imposed by legislation, the statistical picture of decline is even more marked in the case of nonwhite immigrants. One set of figures can dramatize this point. The peak of immigration in any one year for Chinese was 39,579 in 1882, but the quota enacted in 1924 permits entry of only one hundred Chinese per year. In general the decline of first generation immigrants gives rise to an ethnically more homogeneous American population and facilitates the process of assimilation to a common-core American culture.

The story of the immigrant's assimilation, already hinted at, is too familiar to be elaborated at length. With singular poignancy, Oscar Handlin has portrayed how the newcomers ascended the rungs of the economic ladder, and how they became a part of American society in the fullest sense. While many intended to stay only temporarily, they did not for long remain sojourners, but lost their strangeness and adopted the ways of life and thought made familiar to them through the process of accommodation and assimilation.[52] And, as someone has observed, "nothing is more Yankee than a Yankeeized person of foreign descent." The "third-generation" considers itself Ameri-

[51] *Op. cit.*, p. 20.
[52] *Race and Nationality in American Life* (Boston: Little, Brown & Company, 1957), p. 236.

can. Like the sands of time, immigrant cultures disintegrate. One student of the problem noted that the speed of disintegration has been accelerated, particularly among the Germans— one of the more persistent nationality groups: "The German press is rapidly dying. Most German churches have long since given up their services in the German language, and German societies of every description find it increasingly difficult to maintain their membership." [53]

Marcus Hansen, perhaps the most acute student of immigrant life, depicted the weakening of the hold of Old World languages in the immigrant church, signalizing the erosion of ethnic ties:

Much of the history of language revolves about the church, and the transformation can be followed most clearly in congregational and synodical records. . . . In Protestant denominations, where local autonomy permitted the organization to proceed along national lines, foreign speech was more firmly intrenched and change was slower. A city with a large immigrant population might possess separate Lutheran churches for the Germans, Swedes, Danes, and Norwegians. Though they had in common the Augsburg Confession, each clung jealously to its own language and special ways, to such an extent, indeed, that eventually the *youth rebelled*. A home awaited them in the English-speaking Lutheran church which had existed from the early nineteenth century. And when the drift started, the non-English groups were obliged to make *concessions*— both as to language and as to strictness of doctrine. The process was hastened by the World War, and today the transformation is almost complete.[54]

While this process was passing before their very eyes, various students of American life began to haggle over its essence. In

<hr>

[53] Samuel Koenig, "Second and Third Generation Americans," in *One America*, eds. Francis J. Brown and Joseph S. Roucek (Engelwood Cliffs, N. J.: Prentice-Hall, Inc., 1945) , p. 472. Cf. Maurice Davie, "Our Vanishing Minorities," *ibid.*
[54] *The Immigrant and American History* (Cambridge, Mass.: Harvard University Press, 1940) , p. 146. Also cf. Marcus Hansen, *The Problem of the Third Generation Immigrant* (Rock Island, Ill.: Augustana Historical Society, 1938) .

general the line formed in support of either the "melting pot" or the "nation of nations" theory. Cultural pluralists, disturbed by the implications of the melting-pot idea, began to rebel. Our discussion began with some attention to the cultural pluralists. Hence it is fitting that this chapter conclude by resuming the earlier discussion.

Never fully resolved was the debate between the melting-pot notion and the nation of nations concept. It was merely laid aside and largely forgotten. Note that immigrant writers themselves introduced the terms and largely carried on the debate. The idea of America as a "melting pot" of diverse ethnic strands was originally presented by Israel Zangwill in a play, which was performed in Washington, D.C. in 1909 and dedicated to Theodore Roosevelt. Its yearnings and expectations are vividly expressed in these lines:

America is God's Crucible, the great Melting Pot where all the races of Europe are melting and reforming! . . . Here you stand in your fifty groups, with your fifty languages and histories, and your fifty blood hatreds and rivalries. But you won't be long like that, brothers, for these are the fires of God you've come to—these are the fires of God. A fig for your feuds and vendettas! Germans and Frenchmen, Irishmen and Englishmen, Jews and Russians—into the Crucible with you all! God is making the American. . . . The real American . . . will be the fusion of all races.[55]

The cultural pluralism school is frequently associated with Horace Kallen; its revised form as "a nation of nations" was coined by another immigrant Louis Adamic.[56] In general, cultural pluralists encouraged the preservation of cultural values and ethnic patterns which have been transplanted to these shores. Sensitive to the pride of distinct heritages, they feared

[55] *The Melting Pot* (New York: The Macmillan Company, 1909).
[56] Kallen, *Culture and Democracy in the United States* (New York: Boni & Liveright, 1924); and Adamic, *A Nation of Nations* (New York: Harper & Brothers, 1945). Also cf. Adamic, *From Many Lands* (New York: Harper & Brothers, 1940).

46

the dominance implied in the melting-pot notion. Their view presupposes cultural hetcrogeneity—the coexistence of a multiplicity of co-equal cultures, or the patchwork of many cultures. Serious doubts are cast on this theory in view of the operation of assimilation processes earlier reviewed. The logical extreme of cultural pluralism is illustrated in the attempts of certain German groups to form a "German state" in southern Illinois, Wisconsin, or even Texas.[57] Needless to say, these efforts failed. At length even *der deutsche Geist* diminished.

Observe that neither theory is free from the odor of special pleading—the one for a free policy of immigration, since alleged differences would soon be absorbed, and the other for toleration and the freedom to be different.[58] Lately, a third view has come into the picture. Coined by George Stewart, it was picked up by Will Herberg, whose interpretation of the current religious revival hinges so much on the plight of the third-generation immigrants. This is the idea of the "transmuting pot" which seeks to avoid the errors of both the assimilationists and the pluralists. Stewart contends that:

As the foreign elements, a little at a time, were added to the pot, they were not merely melted, but were largely transmuted. . . . Their racial background was of course unchanged, but *culturally and psychologically they generally became American.*[59]

In the transmuting pot all the ingredients are transformed and assimilated to an idealized "Anglo-Saxon model." As differences are reduced through transmutation, one might expect that ethnic churches, which were largely transplanted from the European "spirit of nationalism," would find their former cultural source vanishing. Hence Swedish, German, Dutch, Danish,

[57] Cf. John A. Hawgood, *The Tragedy of German-America* (New York: G. P. Putnam's Sons, 1940), pp. 93-224.

[58] For an excellent discussion of the unifying and discordant tendencies of various nativist and Americanization movements cf. John Higham, *Strangers in the Land* (New Brunswick, N. J.: Rutgers University Press, 1955).

[59] From: *American Ways of Life,* by George R. Stewart. Copyright 1954 by George R. Stewart. Reprinted by permission of Doubleday & Company, Inc.

and Norwegian churches would no longer be able to depend upon an ethnic base for their existence; instead these ethnic churches would share in the common cultural pattern, which provides the new social source for church unity, thereby replacing the erstwhile tendency toward proliferation.

This development bears further examination in later chapters. For the time being, we may note one sign of assimilation in the declining number of non-English speaking churches. Such a process, wherein English supplants the foreign language, is clearly discernible within Congregational Christian churches —a denomination not particularly noted for its ethnic diversity.

TABLE 5

NON-ENGLISH SPEAKING CONGREGATIONAL-CHRISTIAN
CHURCHES, 1930-1955 [60]

Year	Number
1930	577
1935	545
1940	534
1945	455
1950	378
1955	294

The steadily decreasing number of non-English speaking churches shown in Table 5 suggests the pattern of assimilation operating in the evolution toward greater cultural unity within Congregational-Christian churches.

[60] *Yearbook of Congregational-Christian Churches,* 1930, 1935, 1940, 1945, 1950, 1955.

2. Signs of Growing Cultural Unity

Many and varied are the social patterns of American life. These persistent, relatively stable and organized patterns of social relationships are woven into our daily existence often without conscious recognition on our part. In considering patterns of social life which are conducive to cultural unity we shall deal with the following: (1) mass communications, (2) common values, (3) styles of life, (4) mutual dependence, (5) organizational revolution, and (6) symbols of national unity.

I. MASS COMMUNICATIONS

Mass media have become one of the pervasive new patterns of American culture. To say that we live in an age of mass communication is now a truism. For hardly any normal person could —or more significantly, would want to—escape daily contact with TV, radio, newspaper, movies, magazines, comics, or pocket books. Television, sometimes dubbed the "lusty child of the arts," is largely a phenomenon of the past decade; yet one program can now reach 60,000,000 people.[1] In 1956, television was found in 75 per cent of America's households; a figure doubtless higher now, but vast when compared to 12 per cent for 1950.[2]

---

[1] The United States Senate Sub-Committee on Juvenile Delinquency, in its hearings on TV, reported that children of elementary-school age spend on the average twenty-two to twenty-seven hours per week viewing TV. This is roughly the same amount of time spent in the classroom.

[2] United States Census Bureau, "News Release" (July 29, 1956).

Before the triumph of television, radio broadcasting had increased at a very rapid rate as table 6 reveals:

TABLE 6
GROWTH IN RADIO BROADCASTING [3]

Year	Standard Radio Broadcasting Stations	Radio Sets In Use	Per cent of Total U. S. Homes With Radio
1922	30	——————	—
1925	530	3,000,000	8
1940	765	45,300,000	77
1949	1,867	80,000,000	94

By 1950, 95.7 per cent of the dwelling units in the United States were equipped with radios, compared to 8 per cent in 1925. Its phenomenal twentieth-century development has made this medium a common household commodity across the country. Rapid strides made in the radio and television fields have enabled wider common exposure to mass media content for the American public.

Note that just fifty years ago radio, television, motion pictures, and mass circulation magazines were virtually unknown.[4] A veritable twentieth-century revolution has occurred, for now they form part of our way of life. Americans today spend much of their leisure time engrossed with one or another of the mass media. In fact, the average adult spends an estimated quarter of his waking hours engaged in mass media pursuits.

One of the most widespread forms of mass communication is the *daily newspaper*. Let us consider some of the changes wrought in the newspaper industry.

[3] Malone, *op. cit.*, p. 113.

[4] Fifty years ago, the first magazine reached the million mark. Today over forty-six magazines have a circulation of more than a million copies each. Yet on December 15, 1956, Crowell-Colliers suspended the publication of the eighty-three-year-old *Woman's Home Companion*—even though the magazine had 4,000,000 subscribers, it lost $7,500,000 in 1956. Cf. Theodore Peterson, *Magazines in the Twentieth Century* (Urbana, Ill.: University of Illinois Press, 1957).

Various studies document shifts toward concentration.[5] The number of daily newspapers fell from 2,600 in 1909 to 1,750 in 1945. These newspapers were published in some 1,300 cities of which only 117 have competing dailies. Such *lessening of competition* largely resulted from the merger and consolidation of once competing papers. Both the number of newspapers and the competition among them has diminished. Newspaper chains, press associations, and feature syndicates are commonplace in the industry today. While the number of dailies has steadily decreased, the general circulation has rapidly increased. From 1918 to 1944, the total number of all dailies declined 19.4 per cent, while their total circulation jumped 60.4 per cent. New York City provides a vivid example of this trend. In the 1840's sixteen dailies were available to a population of 400,000. In 1950 seven papers served a population that had expanded twenty-fold to approximately 8,000,000.

Growth of one-publisher communities and daily chains has proceeded at a rapid rate since the beginning of the present century, paralleling mergers and consolidations in other walks of life (i.e., business, education, labor, local churches and denominations). In view of the rising costs of competition and the added overhead in maintaining separate staffs, countless newspapers have faced the alternative of "death or consolidation." As a result of co-operative affiliations, newspapers have gained greater economic stability; in turn, the public has increasingly been fed a diet of standardized news.

Attempts to evaluate the effects of the American public's pervasive contact with the mass media have led to various viewpoints. In general the more impressionistic students of society tend to see great influences, while the more "empirically

---

[5] Raymond Nixon, "Concentration and Absenteeism in Daily Newspaper Ownership," *Reader in Public Opinion and Communication*, eds. B. Berelson and M. Janowitz (Chicago: The Free Press of Glencoe, Ill., 1953), pp. 193-207; Paul Neurath, "One-Publisher Communities: Factors Influencing Trend," *Journalism Quarterly*, XXI (September, 1944), 230-42; William Weinfeld, "The Growth of Newspaper Chains in the United States," *Journalism Quarterly*, XIII (December, 1936), 357-80.

oriented" tend to be cautious, if not skeptical. Of the former observers, C. Wright Mills concluded: " (1) The media tell the man in the mass who he is—they give him identity; (2) they tell him what he wants to be—they give him aspirations; (3) they tell him how to get that way—they give him technique, (4) they tell him how to feel that he is that way even when he is not—they give him escape." [6] In the complex network of inter-personal relations, the mass media give orientation to life, provide a framework of understanding, and afford norms for behavior. There are other observers who indignantly deplore the conforming influences of the mass media.[7]

On the other hand, many communications researchers contend that mass media have little *direct* influence on behavior. People are said to select the media content which accords with their own likes and dislikes.[8] After all, this argument runs, influences are exaggerated, since the mass media provide a convenient and highly visible target for criticism.

Between these two diverse viewpoints lie mediating positions and other considerations which bear directly on our theme of cultural unity. Thus the late Louis Wirth, who cannot easily be located in either camp, argued that the press, TV, radio, and movies may become the basis for a new consensus in American society—a new "superculture based on *common exposure* to common ideas." [9] This view gains some support from a study of the urban community press, which concludes that the com-

[6] *The Power Elite*, p. 314. For a discussion of the role of human interest stories in unifying the nation, cf. Helen MacGill Hughes, "Human Interest Stories and Demorcacy," *Reader in Public Opinion and Communication,* eds. Berelson and Janowitz, *op. cit.,* pp. 317-26.

[7] Cf. Frederic Wertham, *Seduction of the Innocent* (New York: Rinehart & Company, 1954) , and Ferderic Wertham, *Circle of Guilt* (New York: Rinehart & Company, 1956) ; and Malcolm Boyd, *Crisis in Communication* (Garden City, N. Y.: Doubleday and Company, 1957) .

[8] Joseph Klapper, *The Effects of Mass Media* (New York: Columbia University, Bureau of Applied Social Research, 1949) .

[9] "Consensus and Mass Communications," *American Sociological Review,* 13 (February, 1948) , 1-15.

munity press contributes to integration by de-emphasizing conflict and highlighting the shared values of a community.[10]

To be sure, the variety and quantity from which an individual may select has also increased in the past two or three decades.[11] Increased selectivity tends to promote specialized audiences and interest groups. Conceivably, parallel to the growth of wider opportunities for choice, there has also developed common frames of reference by which large numbers of people make selections. The point to press, however, is that as a rule people living in Muncie, Indiana, are exposed to relatively the same content as those living in Walla Walla, Washington. Common exposure to the mass media spans sectional differences, racial, ethnic, and class levels. Be they rich or poor, television viewers have generally the same range of choice open to them. Just how much consensus issues from the sharing of common experiences and common exposure seems problematical.[12]

One can hardly deny, however, that the rapid and widespread development of mass communications gives American society a "permeable character" and diminishes the possibility of isolated local communities. Hence George R. Stewart, novelist and professor of English at the University of California, observes a direct influence on the unifying of the English language as spoken in America. He attributes the breakdown of regional dialects to the impact of the mass media:

Even fifty years ago a child might grow up in a southern town, seldom be twenty miles away from it, and rarely hear any speech

[10] Morris Janowitz, *The Community Press in an Urban Setting* (Chicago: The Free Press of Glencoe, Ill., 1952).

[11] Many critics, however, point to the homogenized fare to meet an average of tastes. Cf. Bernard Rosenberg and David M. White, eds., *Mass Culture* (Chicago: The Free Press of Glencoe, Ill., 1957); and Ralph Ross and Ernest van den Haag, *The Fabric of Society* (New York: Harcourt, Brace and Company, 1957).

[12] Some scholars have no hesitation in establishing a direct role of mass media in furthering consensus. Especially cf. Karl Mannheim, *Man and Society in an Age of Reconstruction* (New York: Harcourt Brace and Company, 1940), pp. 129 ff. and Karl Mannheim, *Systematic Sociology* (London: Routledge & Kegan Paul, Ltd., 1957), p. 107.

except that of the neighborhood. Now a southern child is likely to have radio, TV, and motion picture and on them all will hear mostly a dialect that is not his local one. . . . Isolation is the mother of dialects and the South is now no longer isolated.

As a result of the tremendously unifying effect of modern means of communication, we may therefore consider it likely that the language of the United States . . . will become more and more unified.[13]

In Stewart's judgment, the dialects of the various regions in the United States are less pronounced than the different dialects found within France or even Great Britain.[14] This fact is significant, for sociologists have traditionally regarded language as an index of acculturation. A common language, which serves as a stabilizing factor, has been assimiliated by successive waves of immigrant groups fanning out into various sections of the nation. Such a unified language provides one clue for emerging national unity, as the mass media function in part to reduce the variety of distinctive dialects.

Response to similar stimuli knits people together. The frequency of the use of the term "American public" suggests the awareness of a considerable degree of integration, for a public is not a crowd or a mob.[15] A public presupposes common orientation and common reaction, however tenuous such social integration may be.

In subsequent chapters, we will have occasion to deal with the role of common exposure in the development of consensus among Protestants. Also to be explored are the churches' use of the media—particularly in relation to the policy of major networks, which offer sustaining time to representative, united Protestant groups. Our discussion of mass communications may conclude with these observations. The mass media afford a phase of social life not widely shared or present at the turn of

[13] *Op. cit.*, pp. 32-33.
[14] *Ibid.*
[15] Herbert Blumer, "The Mass, the Public and Public Opinion," Berelson and M. Janowitz, *op. cit.*, p. 47.

the century; common exposure takes place on a scale hitherto unknown; mass communication constitutes one contributing factor to the reduction of social differences between groups, as permeability is facilitated; the mass media have a bearing on the dissemination and shaping of similar frames of reference, common orientation, and value themes to which we turn our attention next.

II. COMMON VALUES

Common value themes constitute another pattern of American life. Some students of American society single out cultural values as the most important source for providing consensus.[16]

For our purposes, values may be defined as shared patterns of belief and behavior which imply a sense of preference and are "meaningful, emotion-laden principles" that guide human action.[17] They are the "assumptions by which we live" and around which attitudes are oriented. "Freedom," "individualism," "democracy," and "success" are some typical examples of cultural values, which claim wide allegiance and direct human conduct. Being widely shared, values shape prevailing practices and constitute an important aspect of cultural unity. Concerning the existence of "value consensus" in American culture, Robin Williams wrote:

It is a definite impression of this study that the unity of American value-systems is commonly and seriously *under*estimated. . . . Commonality of values is . . . a matter of belief that there is consensus—not that there is agreement upon the detailed content of every norm and value. Underneath the external flux . . . there are substantial common themes. . . .[18]

Yet one must confess that in dealing with cultural values, one

[16] Robert C. Angell, *Free Society and Moral Crisis* (Ann Arbor: University of Michigan Press, 1958), p. 24; and Williams, *op. cit.*, pp. 518-19, 528, and *passim*.
[17] *Ibid.*, p. 375. In this context, values are not considered in the economic, ethical, or ontological senses.
[18] *Ibid.*, p. 545.

works with an elusive concept. Not only is the content and meaning of values (e.g., freedom) imprecise, but also considerable conflict exists among them; particular values may have greater appeal at certain times and places. Despite this situation of complexity, however, both popular experience and students of society have affirmed widely shared value themes.

In popular parlance, various terms refer to this phenomenon: "American dream," "American creed," "American way of life," "American spirit," and "American promise." These expressions are sometimes vaguely employed; they doubtless convey slightly different connotations. Taken as a whole, they tend to "hang together" and are sufficiently sturdy to provide the basis for a common framework of understanding.[19]

For example, the American dream is largely interpreted as success, "getting ahead in life," security, monetary rewards.[20] When approached and asked about "common value themes," the "average man in the street" may be unable to tick them off readily. This does not destroy the belief that they form part of the ethos of American life, however. On the other hand, our mythical man in the street may be so familiar with American values that he takes them for granted or treats them as clichés. As Ralph Bunche observed:

> Every man in the street, white, black, red, or yellow, knows that this is the "land of the free," the "land of opportunity," the "cradle of liberty," and the "home of democracy"; that the American flag symbolizes the "equality of all men" and guarantees to us all freedom of speech, freedom of religion, and racial tolerance.[21]

[19] This view does not imply that values are static, that they resist social change, or that they do not conflict with one another. Despite conflict there is sufficient over-all agreement, lest the situation be chaotic. For a discussion of value conflict cf. Robert Lynd, *Knowledge For What* (Princeton University Press, 1939); and John Cuber and Robert Harper, *Problems of American Society* (New York: Henry Holt and Company, 1949).

[20] Cf. Robert K. Merton, "Social Structure and Anomie," *Social Theory and Social Structure* (Chicago: The Free Press of Glencoe, Ill., 1957), pp. 136 ff. For a discussion of the American creed cf. Gunnar Myrdal, *An American Dilemma* (New York: Harper & Brothers, 1944), pp. 8-25.

[21] Quoted by Myrdal, *Ibid.* p. 4.

Despite the disharmonies and variations among values, there likely exists a "strain toward consistency"—a tendency for cultural values to support each other, to seek compatibility and congruence with the constituent parts of a society.

Various students of society have sought to identify the common value themes of American culture.[22] Their compiled lists indicate broad areas of agreement. Since there is less than precise definition of values and some degree of conflict among them, it seems best to regard these value themes as "central tendencies," containing relative, rather than absolute, consistency. Of the various compilations, Robin Williams' stands out as the most complete and convincing. His lucid discussion is informed by the writings of American scholars and by such European observers as De Tocqueville, Bryce, Siegfried, Laski, Muller-Freienfels, and Myrdal. Williams sets forth these major value themes: [23]

1. Achievement and success
2. Activity and work
3. Moral orientation
4. Humanitarian *mores*
5. Efficiency and practicality
6. Progress
7. Material comfort
8. Equality
9. Freedom
10. External conformity
11. Science and secular rationality
12. Nationalism and patriotism

[22] Cf. Cuber and Harper, *op. cit.*, p. 368; Angell, *op. cit.*, p. 22; Myrdal, *op. cit.*, pp. 8-10; Commager, *op. cit.*; Max Lerner, *America as a Civilization* (New York: Simon and Schuster, Inc., 1957), pp. 67-71; Lee Coleman, "What is an American: A Study of Alleged American Traits," *Social Forces*, XIX (May, 1941), 498.

[23] *Op. cit.*, pp. 372-442. There is no need here to detail these value themes, since they will be discussed in a later context, and as they contribute to various forms of church unity. For an outsider's view which is nearly identical with Williams' cf. Andre Maurois, "The American Mentality," *The Old and the New World* (Paris: UNESCO, 1956), p. 321. For a list of contradictory value clichés cf. Lynd, *op. cit.*, pp. 60-63.

13. Democracy
14. Individual personality

The evidence that these values have undergone radical change is meager. With the exception of science and secular rationality, value themes perhaps remain not too different from those prevailing at the turn of the century. But this observation does not vitiate the present-day function of values as one of the persistent patterns contributing to national unity.

A provocative recent study of changing values among college students points to the relative durability of value patterns. In a sweeping conclusion based on a composite summary of five surveys of various college populations, the author claimed:

American college students tend to think alike, feel alike, and believe alike. To an extraordinary degree, their values are the same wherever they may be studying and whatever the stage of their college careers. . . . 75 to 80% of American college students fit a "common mold" in allegiance to similar values, regardless of location, type of administration, size of student body, or character of the educational program.[24]

Even if one grants that these findings, which prompted lively discussion in academic circles, are only partially correct, they suggest the profound conditioning power of a common ethos, and the ability of different institutions of our society to inculcate similar value themes. Thus the most dramatic change is perhaps found in the wider sharing of value themes. Instead of being largely confined to an elite "leisure class," values now enjoy wider consensus and greater assimilation by all classes, ethnic groups, and people living in various parts of the nation.

Frequently the major value themes of American society are associated with a middle-class, bourgeois mentality. Perhaps the middle class is more articulate in advancing them and more

[24] Philip E. Jacob, *Changing Values in College* (New Haven: Edward W. Hazen Foundation, 1956), pp. 5, 14. For critiques of this study, cf., John E. Smith, *Value Convictions and Higher Education* (New Haven: Edward W. Hazen Foundation, 1959); and Allen Barton, *Studying the Effects of College Education* (New Haven: Edward W. Hazen Foundation, 1959).

disciplined in observing them. These values, however, tend to form part of the common-core culture, adherence to which cuts across class, racial, sectional, and ethnic lines. Such loyalties contribute to the underlying consensus, and constitute another sign of the unity of American society.

III. STYLES OF LIFE

"Mass culture" increasingly is noted as a pattern of present-day life. Observers point to the emergence of mass media, mass leisure, mass production, mass education, mass advertisement, mass housing, mass reading clubs. Although empirical studies on the nature and variability of the trend toward "massification" are few, there hardly lacks lively discussion of its currency.[25] Most of this discussion centers around the dynamic changes taking place in styles of life, and how these changes have led to "conformity" and "homogeneity of tastes." [26]

Changes in styles of life obviously comprise a very broad theme. For it conceivably includes such items as humor. Indeed Gilbert Highet pointed to the passing of regional and dialect humor and of wisecracks which might be interpreted as racial slurs:

It used to be a very poor Master of Ceremonies who could not tell stories in Irish dialect, Swedish dialect, Italian and Jewish and Scotish and Negro and Spanish dialect. But nowadays if he did such a thing, he would surely receive protests, accusing him of holding his fellow citizens up to ridicule and contempt.[27]

[25] Nearly all the popular commentators on American culture deal with this problem. See the writings of David Riesman, C. Wright Mills, William Whyte, Max Lerner. Sophisticated journals of opinion, such as *Diogenes, Partisan Review, Dissent, Perspectives, Commentary,* and *Encounter* are replete with discussions of this theme.

[26] Critics who decry growing conformity patterns in contemporary life are hard pressed to substantiate these claims. For nineteenth-century village life may well have exacted greater conformity than present-day urban existence. It is likely that the substantive question of what one conforms to is the crucial issue often bypassed in the eagerness to discuss greater or lesser amounts of conformity.

[27] "Modern American Humor" (transcript of a radio talk, reprinted by Book-of-the Month Club, Spring, 1956). Of course there are many factors involved

Generally speaking, styles of life pertain to such common practices as manners,[28] dress, food habits, fashions, and entertainment. The revealing term "taste" is frequently used in speaking of styles of life. For our study several implications may be drawn:

1. A growing consensus in matters of taste does not necessarily indicate less variety from which to choose, but rather a similar frame of reference by which choices are made. An example of this may be taken from our food habits. The American scene is characterized by a myriad richness of food backgrounds, with regional dishes supplemented by ethnic culinary. Opportunities for choice are abundant, and the desire to sample ethnic dishes—for example, chow mein and pizza—or regional ones—Southern fried chicken—is widespread. Hence restaurants serving Chinese or Mexican food or Swedish smörgåsbord are popularly patronized. Nor is it unusual for a family to eat spaghetti on Tuesday and Southern fried chicken with "French fries" on Wednesday. Along with this rich variety also goes greater common acceptance, which encourages common orientation. Consensus in matters of taste suggests a "pervasive signaling of a shared culture." [29]

2. Changes in styles of life do not take place within a vacuum, but they interlace with dynamic social changes taking place in the rest of the social structure. In some instances, they reflect these changes. Consider the growth of the advertising industry or the revolution in leisure time. Advertising, says *Fortune Magazine's* sociological critic Daniel Bell, appeals to "the good life" by teaching people "how to dress, to furnish

in this change in our style of life. Apart from the work of protest organizations and the growing acceptance of ethnic groups as fitting into a common culture, there is the stubborn fact that the ability to imitate dialect correctly is a lost art.

[28] Note the desire to seek a "right way to behave," as evidenced by etiquette books, especially by Emily Post and Amy Vanderbilt. Their works have become "arbiters of American manners," and not solely the property of the so-called leisure class. Between 1920 and 1945, Emily Post's *Etiquette* sold over a million copies.

[29] Williams, *op. cit.*, p. 545.

a home, the wines to put away—in short, the styles of life appropriate to new middle-class status."[30] With respect to leisure, Americans now have it in greater quantity and distributed more widely among various strata of people than at any other time or place in history.[31] Yet not so many decades ago the twelve-hour workday was standard. At least potentially, mass leisure affords greater opportunity and free time for cultivating standards of appreciation and taste in such pursuits as art, music, fashions, and household furnishings.[32]

What bearing do changes in styles of life have on the emerging unity of American culture? Implicitly we have inferred that such changes close the gap between peoples of different ethnic, class, and sectional ties. Examples might help illustrate this trend. A housewife in "Plainville, U.S.A." may wear the latest fashions, little different from those worn by society matrons in "Yankee City" or Paris—as the Dior model is copied on "Seventh Avenue," New York's mass production garment industry, and quickly disseminated throughout the land. Driving a Cadillac was once considered a "badge of success." Now, however, with so many Negroes and members of minority groups driving Cadillacs to display their social advancement, General Motors' deep concern led to the production of even more exclusive models with limited sales.[33]

Increasingly, working-class women use the same kinds of dishwashers and washing machines, and even choose the same wallpaper as do the wives of executives. A best-selling book in New York also registers as a best seller in New Orleans.

---

[30] "The Impact of Advertising," *The New Leader* (February 11, 1957) , 10.

[31] Cf. August Heckscher, *The Twentieth Century Fund, Annual Report* (1956) . A gradual shrinking of the working week in the United States has taken place. In 1850 the working week was 70 hours, 1900—60.2 hours, 1920—49.7 hours, 1940—44 hours, 1955—40.2 hours. There is current discussion that a four-day week, five hours work per day is within the range of possibility.

[32] For the statement of both sides of this issue cf. the first two essays in Rosenberg and White, *op. cit.*, pp. 3-21. It should be recalled that our concern is not with the issue of "vulgarization" or lowering of standards, but rather in pointing out wide dissemination that cuts across class, race, ethnic, and sectional lines and reduces social differences.

[33] Bell, *op. cit.*, p. 10.

People in San Francisco search just as anxiously for coveted tickets to *My Fair Lady* as those in Boston. In short, styles of life are becoming more alike, more often copied, and apply more equally to every sector of the nation, every class, race, and ethnic status. Growing common behavior and attitudes toward styles of life comprise, at the very least, suggestive indicators of growing consensus in American society.

IV. MUTUAL DEPENDENCE

Much of modern life is formed by overlapping circles of interdependence. Individuals and institutions relate to one another in such intricate ways, that interdependence is often taken for granted. When a breakdown or accident occurs, however, this realization comes vividly to the fore. Obvious examples may be selected from almost any of the transportation media—subway, tugboat, train, airplane, shipping, trucking. If one subway train failed to function properly, it would create only slight concern (although sometimes it would tie up a whole line and delay many thousands). But when all the subways in a city like New York fail to operate, serious complications multiply, affecting the work of major institutions—children going to school, employees on their way to work, shoppers out buying, individuals going to some center of entertainment. This single mundane example drawn from one medium of one industry might well be paralleled in many areas of life.

Consider the mutual dependence of the rural dweller with his city cousin, or of the suburbanite with both urban and rural communities. Almost any social function that one conceives of has a complex chain of interdependent relationships—building a house, teaching students, eating at a restaurant.

Compare the present-day interdependence of a "contractural society" with the earlier period of greater independence and self-sufficiency. In various walks of life nineteenth-century, predominantly rural America stands in marked contrast with the mid-twentieth century, basically industrial scene. Contemporary mass urban society has moved toward an ever-closer interdependence. In contrast rural people traditionally depend less upon others for satisfying their basic life needs, including the production of one's own food, clothing, and shelter. Increasing complexity in the modern urban community makes reliance upon the clock and timetable a necessity; whereas life in an agrarian economy proceeds at a pace which is less clock-driven and schedulized. The more recent period is marked by elaborately developed mechanization and technological advances. In short, with increased specialization, men live together in modern cities in relationships that are largely symbiotic, rather than highly personal. Increased functional dependence upon a vast human network is a characteristic feature of present-day society.

The implications of these remarks for cultural unity have been drawn well by the pioneer French sociologist Emile Durkheim, who first analyzed the integrative function of the division of labor.[34] On the surface it appears that the division of labor was an obvious divisive factor, conducive to an infinite amount of social disunity; yet Durkheim's probing analysis suggests that the division of labor may itself function to create unity. For the work of one man—or team—seeks completion in that of another. Without such mutual dependence, serious maladjustments occur in a complex technological society. This process tends to break down patterns of insulation between individual and group; for mutual dependence heightens interaction. Hence the division of labor may lead to the strengthening of social integration in view of the functional interdependence it presupposes.

While mutual dependence may not per se be a sufficient bond to maintain the conscious consensus of a people, it contributes latently to cultural unity. In later chapters, its role will be drawn with respect to ecumenical institutions.

V. ORGANIZATIONAL REVOLUTION

Like the division of labor which characterizes a highly developed, complex industrial society, the proliferation of organi-

[34] *The Division of Labor in Society*, tr. George Simpson (Chicago: The Free Press of Glencoe, Ill., 1947).

zations provides a parallel phenomenon. Kenneth Boulding has called this the "organizational revolution"; another suggestive phrase, coined by Robert C. Angell, is the "nucleation process." [35] Almost all observers of American culture, both foreign and native, have commented on the propensity of Americans to develop voluntary associations. This situation has given rise to the cliché that we are a "nation of joiners bent on belonging." [36] Says the Chicago sociologist Robert E. Park, "What a man belongs to constitutes most of his life career and all of his obituary."

When one compares the extent of organizational development in 1852 with the situation in 1952, he does not wonder that the term "revolution" is fitting. Boulding points out that in 1852 one found practically no labor unions, employer's or trade associations, farm organizations; no American Legion, Department of Agriculture or Labor in the national government; few corporations and large businesses.[37]

Today there exists a "swarming multiplicity" of self-organized groupings and associations—special interest groups from Audubon societies to Zoroastrians. Since many associations keep membership records, ample statistical data are available.[38] The major fraternal orders report a total membership of 20,000,000 persons. Service clubs—Rotary, Lions, Kiwanis, Optimists—number over 9,000, covering the nation with local units in nearly every urban place. Even if a traveling Rotarian misses a meeting in his

---

[35] Boulding, *The Organizational Revolution* (New York: Harper & Brothers, 1953). Angell, *op. cit.*, p. 58.

[36] For a contrary view cf. Charles Wright and Herbert H. Hyman, "Voluntary Association Memberships," *American Sociological Review*, 23 (June, 1958), 284-94.

[37] *Op. cit.*, pp. 3-4. Boulding's claim is all the more striking when it is recalled that over a century ago, Alexis de Tocqueville opined that "in no country in the world has the principle of association been more successfully used, or applied to a greater multitude of objects than in America." Cf., Alexis de Tocquerville, *Democracy in America* (New York: Vintage Books Inc., 1954), p. 198.

[38] Cf. Jay Judkins, *National Associations of the United States* (Washington, D. C.: U. S. Department of Commerce, 1949).

home town, he can, and, indeed, is obligated to, "make it up" practically anywhere he happens to find himself.

Countless college fraternities and business and professional associations abound. The American Medical Association alone has 2,000 county and district societies; women's clubs number in the neighborhood of 100,000; special purpose organizations flourish; for example, 123 *national* organizations in 1945 were working toward improved race relations. And so it goes. It is a rare American, avers the late Charles A. Beard of New Milford, who is not a member of four or five organizations.

Note also the elaboration of such formal organizations as educational and philanthropic foundations, occupational and professional groupings, and large corporate structures and government agencies. Increasingly, individual participation has shifted from the prototype of the democratic town meeting to indirect involvement through representative delegates and organizations. Individual action is channeled through organizational structures in order to exercise effective influence. These large-scale organizations give rise to such commonplace expressions as "big business," "big government," "big farmer," and "big labor."

Another organizational development is the tendency toward increased centralization of both formal and informal organizations. In what he terms the "nucleation process," Robert C. Angell notes this trend:

> Where formerly there were thousands of small towns with small firms related to the local market, there are now in addition, hundreds of large cities with great corporations producing for and distributing to regional, national, and international markets. Although many small units are still operating, they are parts of great networks of production and consumption dominated by units of gigantic size.[39]

The chain-store phenomenon occurs not alone in business. Increasingly it takes place in voluntary associations as well. Nation-

[39] *Op. cit.*, p. 58.

ally affiliated integrated programs reflect this trend in organizations like the National Recreation Association, National Association for Mental Health, National Probation Association, and American Public Welfare Association.

A tendency on the part of individuals to *broaden their organizational loyalties* forms another noticeable trend. Individuals tend to participate with only part of themselves; in this "segmental participation" allegiances are spread over many organizations, rather than intensive involvement in only a few. Rapid developments in the field of organized charity may partly illumine this point.

Disappearing is the day when individual contributions are meted out on a person-to-person basis. Charity has become institutionalized. Individual giving to a general fund which serves a whole host of agencies is prevalent practice. Witness the development of co-ordinated campaign funds and united appeals through community chests and councils. These community chests, operating at the local community level, in turn unite their forces into a national movement. Thus the "United Community Funds and Councils of America" was organized through a national merger of the then existing "Community Chests" and "Community Welfare Councils" in 1918. Membership in this national organization now includes 1,400 local communities. Among other things, it promotes nation-wide publicity—behind the slogan, "Give the United Way"—and advises local units in their relations with private and public agencies. Through its co-ordinated, "teamwork" approach, the national body reports that "in the last twenty-five years the number of Federated Campaigns has grown from 240 to over 2,000, and the total amount raised per year from 58 to 412 million dollars."

Developments in business and voluntary associations have their counterparts in education, labor, and religious institutions, as subsequent chapters will disclose.[40] Co-ordination and

[40] For additional data on mergers cf. Federal Trade Commission, *Report on Corporate Mergers and Acquisitions* (Washington, D. C.: U. S. Government Printing Office, 1955), pp. 1-209; Arthur J. Goldberg, *A.F.L.-C.I.O.: Labor*

centralization lead to concentration of power and elaboration of complicated machinery for administrative purposes. As power centralizes in one institutional sphere, it calls forth "countervailing powers" in other areas. Such nucleation and "counternucleation" seems to be the order of the day for business, government, labor, farming, and churches as well. To anticipate our later discussion, Herbert W. Schneider has called attention to the fact that religion in twentieth-century America is marked by organizations whose outward appurtenances resemble the office buildings of big business, with specialized agencies, boards, and departments, so that the life of religion seems to be "shifting from religious worship to 'service,' and from altar to office." [41]

The development of highly organized and centralized religious organizations reflects the increased dependence upon these agencies for service functions which they perform. It also indicates the parallel development of the organizational revolution in religion as in other walks of life. As J. Milton Yinger put it: "In a day when poultrymen, engineers, and physicians have joined together in their various organizations for a more effective pursuit of their interests, it is not surprising to find religious groups following the same pattern." [42]

What implications for unity may be drawn from the growth of organizations and their tendency to centralize? While it oversimplifies to identify integration with a highly developed organizational life, such developments, in their latent function, contribute to cultural unity.

Increasingly, the co-ordination of organizations means contact between national and local units or chapters. This is particularly true for voluntary associations and fraternities, linked into larger unities with national headquarters. Integra-

United (New York: McGraw Hill Book Company, 1957) ; "Co-operation of the Organized Professions in Social Welfare," Proceedings of Workshop (National Social Welfare Assembly and United Community Funds and Councils of America, 1956) ; Herbert Lehman, "Giant Business Expands," *The New Leader* (April 29, 1957) , 6-7.

[41] *Religion in Twentieth Century America* (Cambridge, Mass.: Harvard University Press, 1952) , p. 24.

[42] *Op. cit.,* p. 293.

tion is encouraged to the extent that these organizations represent interlocking memberships, which embrace different ages, classes, regions, races, and ethnic groups.[43] They foster communication and contact. Many of these groups are oriented to the "common good of the community," and bring together diverse people to pursue limited goals. In the corporate structure, some evidence indicates that both geographical and upward social mobility is fostered.[44]

Perhaps the most decisive consequence is the overlapping membership in various organizations, and the over-all stability this tends to promote. At each point in his life the same man plays many different roles—father, bread winner, club member, union member, neighbor, churchman—in which he conforms to different expectations. Yet his modes of behavior have a way of becoming interlaced, so that conflict is minimized, and the inconsistent demands of his various roles are made relatively compatible.[45] In the process, defining norms of behavior governing one sphere of life are carried over into other organizations.

This occupancy of multiple roles forms a web of interlocking social relationships. Hence participation in many organizations may serve as a *connecting link* between the individual and society. Even the exposure to conflicting viewpoints may heighten the awareness of common goals, as the groups (e.g., labor and management) work out ways of accommodation. The organizational revolution, then, may well function as an integrative and stabilizing factor in the quest for national unity. Its impact

[43] Arthur M. Schlesinger, *Paths to the Present* (New York: The Macmillan Company, 1949), p. 50. Schlesinger regards the multiplicity of organizations as a great cementing force for integration.

[44] *Infra*, chap. VI.

[45] Merton develops this framework of analysis in great detail. Cf. Merton, *op. cit.*, pp. 368-86. For a slightly different approach to this same problem of unity emerging from the multiplicity of organizations cf. Williams, *op. cit.*, p. 529. Williams suggests that an important source of unity comes "directly from diversity" of organizations. The overlapping of groups, the cross-pressures and criss-crossing of allegiances blur the sharp edges and "cancel-out" one another. Hence, Williams contends, the "realistic sociological meaning in the national motto on our coins—*e pluribus unum*."

(particularly the trend toward centralization) on ecumenical institutions will bear further examination in later chapters.

VI. CULTURAL SYMBOLS

Unlike other modern nations with highly visible institutionalized leadership patterns, such as an emperor, a king, or a party, the symbols of national unity in the United States are less easily discernible. Yet, despite its relatively short history, America also has its traditions, its folklore, its heroes, and its "manifest destiny." Seldom is the specific meaning or content of these symbols for national unity well defined. In fact, "many of the most important symbols of national unity have so little specific ideological content that they create a common allegiance by being all things to all men." [46] One might point to the flag, or the Constitution, or the Declaration of Independence, or the national anthem; in some sense they all stimulate national unity. National parks and monuments, national holidays, the celebration of the birthday of a leader, or the observance of critical events in the nation's history—these too serve as symbols of national unity.

Durkheim has called attention to a society's need for "collective representation," and for the reaffirmation at regular intervals of the collective ideas and sentiments which make its unity.[47] Formal occasions are designated and appropriately celebrated with ceremonials to emphasize national unity. They unconsciously renew the apprehension of the nation's significance. Fourth of July, Thanksgiving, Armistice, and Memoral Day come immediately to mind. Even Labor Day serves to emphasize the unity of the nation, rather than to call attention to a special class of proletarians. National observances generally function latently to support national unity.

As if to document Durkheim's principle in a modern American setting, Lloyd Warner's provocative analysis of Me-

---

[46] Williams, *op. cit.*, p. 530.
[47] *The Elementary Forms of the Religious Life*, tr. J. W. Swain (Chicago: The Free Press of Glencoe, 1947).

morial Day ceremonies is noteworthy. According to Warner, Memorial Day ceremonies are rituals of a sacred symbol system which function periodically to unify the entire community:

Memorial Day is a cult of the dead which organizes and integrates the various faiths and national and class groups into a sacred unity. . . . Its principal themes are those of the sacrifice of the soldier dead for the living and the obligation of the living to sacrifice their individual purposes for the good of the group.[48]

Warner analyzes the community's participation and preparation for observance of Memorial Day—the parades, the symbol of the red poppy, the public speeches, and the common involvement of all the churches, culminating in a common ritual at the graveyard observed by Protestant, Catholic, Jewish, and Greek Orthodox alike. In short, though the services pay homage to the dead, their largely unintended consequence is to remind the living of the collective ideals of the nation, to de-emphasize divisive values, and to invoke continued patriotism of all the citizenry, contributing thereby to the community's unity.

As earlier intimated, national holidays function as symbols of national unity. While few changes are reported in the number of observances over the last hundred years, change is apparent at two points. First, national holidays have become more widely diffused. A number of American holidays (e.g., Columbus Day) originated as ethnic or regional celebrations, and then became national in scope and attention. As Stewart maintains:

Historically, most of our holidays have arisen at the instance of particular people or of particular groups. They began little, and grew. As they grew, they tended to escape from special interests and to become more universally and also more vaguely American.[49]

Second, generally speaking, American holidays have been subject to a "leveling" process. The original meaning or reli-

[48] *American Life: Dream and Reality* (Chicago: University of Chicago Press, 1953), p. 3.
[49] *Op. cit.*, p. 271.

gious significance of many national holidays has eroded; hence people share a similar frame of reference with respect to national holidays—they tend to do the same thing on the various holidays and generally regard these events as days when they are free from work.[50]

In addition to these formal symbols and ceremonials of national unity, note the vast array of informal and casual ones, ranging all the way from meaningful occasions to commonplace behavior patterns.

If history, as someone has defined it, is the memory of a people, then Americans are not without their history of common triumphs, sorrows, and disasters which reinforce the bonds of unity.[51] Common external perils serve an important function in galvanizing unity. In fact, the more widely people share the belief that an external danger threatens the nation, the greater their tendency to think alike, to accept a national effort to preserve a way of life.[52] Who can deny the threats imposed from external stimuli in recent times?

Finally, there are the well-nigh countless traits known characteristically as symbols of American life. While devotees of "highbrow culture" may frown, these traits include such things as baseball and hot dogs.[53] Indeed, note that although baseball is called the national pastime, only in the spring of 1958 did the National League become truly national in the geographical

---

[50] *Ibid.*

[51] In this connection, observe the resurgence of interest in the Civil War period, both in historical novels and serious research. Also the current interest in "Westerns," which have become a staple diet of television, might be viewed as a vicarious sharing of frontier hardships along with the "builders" of America. Since the rest of us have played no part in the early molding of the nation on the frontier, we may well identify with these pioneer Americans.

[52] Cf. Samuel A. Stouffer, *Communism, Conformity and Civil Liberties* (Garden City, N. Y.: Doubleday & Company, 1955).

[53] Foreign visitors, including royalty, frequently profess the desire for the experience of eating an American hot dog. Thus it is reported that King George VI and Queen Elizabeth enjoyed hot dogs at a picnic given by President and Mrs. Roosevelt at Hyde Park, during which King George, in asking for a second, commented on "this delightful hot-dog sandwich." Other foodstuffs which are cited as symbols of the American way of life include blueberry pie, ham and eggs, and turkey—the latter is particularly associated with the Thanksgiving meal.

71

sense. When the Brooklyn Dodgers and the New York Giants, erstwhile inhabitants of the Brooklyn and Bronx Boroughs, relocated in California, major league baseball penetrated west of the Rockies. Now the national pastime in its major league form spans the continent from the East to the West Coast.[54]

In American popular culture, the common symbols and type-figures who serve as folk heroes—the ball player and the entertainer of stage and screen—do not necessarily conform to ethnic, sectional, or class lines. Willy Mays, Frank Sinatra, Elvis Presley, or Sammy Davis, Jr., in the popular mind, are national symbols that cut across these barriers. Thus national symbols, formal and informal, foster national unity by evoking common memories, collective ideas, and shared loyalties. Community is experienced, in part, through participation in common symbols. These symbols have become more widely shared and tend to promote similar frames of reference, thereby constituting an index of emerging cultural unity. The symbolic function of ecumenical institutions will receive some attention in subsequent chapters.

VII. SUMMARY

A mere enumeration of social trends is sufficient for deriving a picture of the dynamic processes and patterns at work in American society, and for summarizing the general concern of the last two chapters:

1. Inflamed feelings engendered by two world wars, including struggles against the country of national origin in many cases, have reinforced loyalties to America. In several instances, as with the Slovaks and Croats, the tragedies of war rendered nationality groups "nationless." In other nations, where Communism has gained the ascendency, loyalties to the old country have also faded fast.

2. Succeeding generations, through education and wider community contacts, have largely adopted and come to prefer the

[54] Geographical distribution on a wider scale also occurred earlier in 1953, when the Boston Braves shifted to Milwaukee; and in the American League, the Philadelphia Athletics also joined the westward procession, transferring to Kansas City in 1954.

ethos of the larger community. Allegiance to a common culture tends to replace solidarity once rooted in ethnic sources.

3. A common language unified the various tongues, and the ability to converse in the mother tongue was lost or concealed.

4. Comparative economic well-being with a chance to "build a better life" strengthened attachments to this adopted land. As Jean de Crevecoeur once wrote, "Where there is bread, there is my country!"

5. Relative freedom of intermarriage across ethnic lines, and incidentally, across denominational lines, tended to disrupt both ethnic and denominational isolation.

6. Transition from rural patterns to urbanization broke down patterns of rural insulation and tended to reduce ethnic visibility through the new prevailing patterns of indifference or anonymity in the urban environment.

7. Our dynamic industrial society necessitates and fosters a more interdependent and integrated functioning culture.

8. Absorption of common value themes through organizational participation and wider exposure to mass media content and similar styles of life contribute to consensus.

9. Identity with the symbols and values of national unity on a formal and informal basis is conducive to a common frame of reference.

10. Greater unity is imposed by the reduction of social differences along class, sectional, racial, and ethnic lines.

These social considerations—embraced under a discussion of the processes and patterns of unity—provide sufficient evidence to indicate definite trends of an emerging cultural unity of American society. Each of the diverse factors, if taken alone, would probably not yield such a conclusion. But functioning in concert and viewing their cumulative impact, the conclusion that these trends exert an influence toward an emerging cultural unity is well-nigh irresistible. The role that this cultural unity bears in relation to the institutional expressions of church unity will presently be our concern.

The discussion in Part I has dealt at one level with the thesis of the social sources of church unity. It was based on the assumption that if an emerging unity in American society could be documented, largely through the development of new phases of social change, the interpretive grounds for the divisive influences of social sources would be seriously undermined. In the context of a dynamic society the diversities of American life—the variant national, social, sectional, and racial marks of identification—have been joined together in unprecedented fashion. One might say that the realization of cultural similarity has never been so widely extended in American life.

If social divisiveness has diminished, then the churches are hard-pressed to prove that continuing divisions are due to the divided state of the social order. For the social conditions which spawned proliferation in church and society are rooted in a social structure which is largely altered; and hence less apt to provide the same occasion for church disunity. Indeed, one suspects that holding social factors responsible for the existing schisms obscures underlying issues, and that religious groups hide behind such explanations to resist ecumenicity.

Earlier forms of church division become inappropriate instruments for reflecting the new cultural unity. In light of the changed social context, one might expect to find the emergence of new ecumenical institutions and the intensification of existing ones. If the proliferation of religious groups is due to the fragmenting influences of American society, then religious unity may spring from cultural unity. This possibility awaits further examination, as we consider the role of social factors in the institutional arrangements of church unity.

Part II seeks to analyze the role of cultural unity in relation to church unity. Chapter III in Part II deals with some preliminary signs of church unity in the present century. In some ways, it furnishes background material, against which succeeding chapters may be viewed. Two sections comprise this first chapter of Part II. The first deals with the formation of the Federal Council of Churches. Section two documents the components of a "common-core Protestantism."

PART TWO

THE SIGNS OF CHURCH UNITY

3. Expressions of Church Unity

At first glance it would appear that the movement for church unity has made little headway in the United States. Since American Christianity can still be divided into some 258 "varieties" of religious groups, the argument that the divisive tendencies have been checked seems weak. Upon probing, however, the apparent diversity of religious life in America is less impressive. Numerically, the religious groups have remained fairly constant (the *Yearbook of American Churches* for 1926 reports 263 groups), while the proportion of church members has increased phenomenally. Compared to the increased membership of the Christian churches, there have been progressively fewer denominations. The ratio is as follows:

One religious group for every 170,500 adult members in 1906.

One religious group for every 207,500 adult members in 1926.

One religious group for every 400,000 adult members in 1956.

In addition, the statistics may be misleading; for 98.4 per cent of the total membership can be located in eighty-two groups, and 75 per cent of the non-Roman Catholic Christians are identified with five major denominational families. Methodism alone claims twenty-two bodies, but one of them contains seven eighths of the total Methodist membership.[1] Many exceedingly small groups flourish; over forty have fewer than 1,000 members each. The combined membership of 140 groups

[1] In 1957 there were ten groups of Presbyterians, fourteen varieties of Mennonites, and twenty-seven types of Baptists.

totals less than one half of 1 per cent of the entire Protestant constituency.

Although an outside observer may still view the American religious scene as an "ecclesiastical zoo exhibiting all sorts of religious wild life," the significant new fact of twentieth-century Protestantism is a shifting pattern of ascendant religious unity.

The signs of unity, measured by any reasonable test, are quite remarkable.[2] Discussions today take place not merely among personal friends, but also involve denominationally delegated representatives. Large numbers of churchmen from scores of denominations and church agencies participate in ecumenical affairs. Growing is the sense of willingness to deal with the crucial issues of faith and order. In this respect, the Oberlin Conference on Faith and Order—the first of its kind held on American soil in the summer of 1957—is a significant landmark. Contrast the present-day situation with the turn of the century, when "in 1900, despite the influence of men like Schaff and Huntington, no churches were formally discussing unity—not to speak of union." [3] Consider Henry Van Dusen's stunning observation:

Just a hundred and fifty years ago you could have traveled this earth from end to end and you would not have discovered one group of any kind, minister, laymen, men or women of different denominations banded together as Christians—not one. But today, thousands of interdenominational organizations in the United States alone . . . work together.[4]

Yet American church history is not without its advocates for church unity almost from the very beginning. Proposals go

[2] We shall not discuss the field of journalism, the many signs of topical interest in ecumenicity among religious journals and periodicals, and recent books on church unity. The growing body of ecumenical literature testifies to the self-consciousness of the movement as an outstanding mark of our religious situation. Of great significance are the series of books published under the William Henry Hoover Lectureship on Christian Unity.

[3] Henry Smith Leiper, "Reunion and the Ecumenical Movement," in *Protestant Thought in the Twentieth Century*, ed. Arnold S. Nash, (New York: The Macmillan Company, 1951), p. 267.

[4] "A New Day in the World Church," *World Outlook* (May, 1957), p. 303.

back at least as far as the 1600's with John Eliot in the deep New England woods.[5] His plans, as well as other sporadic attempts, failed to take root. Various scattered efforts at church unity yielded few permanent results until the nineteenth century, when such movements as the following were launched. The American Board of Commissioners for Foreign Missions started in 1810 under Congregational, Presbyterian, and Dutch Reformed Auspices. Later, in 1870, due to resurgent denominational consciousness, the Board became wholly Congregational, as the Presbyterians and then the Reformed developed their own societies for foreign missions. The American Bible Society, founded in 1816, included the support of Presbyterians, Congregationalists, Episcopalians, Baptists, Methodists, Dutch Reformed, and Friends. The Sunday School Movement by 1872 provided uniform lesson materials. The Young Men's Christian Association came to America in 1855, followed soon by the Young Women's Christian Association. The American branch of the Evangelical Alliance began in 1867. The Young People's Society of Christian Endeavor started in 1881. The Foreign Missions Conference in North America organized in 1893. During the century, not a few proposals for church union received a hearing: S. S. Schmucker, a Lutheran, made a vigorous appeal for "Catholic Union" in 1836; Thomas Hubbard Vail in 1841, William Augustus Muhlenberg in 1853, and William Reed Huntington in 1870 all advocated plans.

Despite all these advances, one would hardly claim that church unity flourished among American Protestants in the nineteenth century. On balance, one might conclude that it was a period characterized more by disunity and fragmentation, a time marked by hyper-denominational emphasis. Sectarianism seethed in the expanding frontier; tides of immigrant groups; splits over the slavery issue, which affected every major denomination; dissension over forms of church government; bitter rivalries and acrimonious debates cut deeply into church life.

[5] Robert S. Bilheimer, *The Quest for Christian Unity* (New York: Association Press, 1952), p. 25.

77

Sectarianism, wrote Huntington, was the "almost universal state of mind in the United States of 1869." [6] During the first three decades of the last century, "substantially every older denomination . . . experienced a schism due to the fact that the main body could not keep up with the more radical spirit of the frontier."[7] Hence despite significant strides toward unity in the nineteenth century, still more persistent undercurrents of "schismatic differentiation" swirled about.

I. FEDERAL COUNCIL OF CHURCHES

In the twentieth century church unity developed with an accelerated tempo and gained greater extension and deeper significance. In fact, Samuel McCrea Cavert, one of the pioneer leaders, contends, "The whole course of what we call the ecumenical movement has taken place within fifty years. My generation has seen it all." [8] A fresh apprehension of a goal, often obscured in the past, began to assume stable institutional roots.

The founding of the Federal Council of Churches in 1908 conveniently marks the turning point in the road to unity, and becomes the first great sign of that growing unity. Conceived as a federation of the national bodies of the churches, the Council declared its main purposes: "To manifest the essential oneness of the Christian churches of America in Jesus Christ as their Divine Lord and Saviour" and "To secure a *larger combined influence for the churches of Christ in all matters affecting the moral and social condition of the people,* so as to promote the *application of the law of Christ in every relation of human life."* Its increased budget furnishes one clue to the scope and expansion of the Council's activities. In 1909, the amount was 9,000

[6] Stephen Neill and Ruth Rouse, *A History of the Ecumenical Movement* (Philadelphia: the Westminster Press, 1954), p. 258. For other evidence of disunity cf. Peter Mode, *The Frontier Spirit in American Christianity* (New York: The Macmillan Company, 1923). But for a contrary view cf. Winthrop Hudson, *The Great Tradition of the American Churches* (New York: Harper & Brothers, 1953).

[7] H. Paul Douglass, *Church Unity Movements in the United States* (New York: Institute of Social and Religious Research, 1934), p. 33.

[8] "The Ecumenical Movement: Retrospect and Prospect," *Ecumenical Review* (April, 1958), p. 313.

dollars, but by 1948, the figure had risen to 649,644 dollars. The Council grew to become the largest church federation in the world.[9]

Why did the Federal Council's effort at interdenominational co-operation succeed when so many previous attempts had failed?

The *role of social factors* is worth noting in this connection. Early twentieth-century economic and social changes constitute a potent influence—particularly the problems precipitated by urbanization and the plight of the city's churches. In his account of the Federal Council, John A. Hutchison observes, "City life, combined with new currents of scientific and technological thought, produced an increasingly powerful secularism; and to meet this new force, the churches found *union* necessary." [10] The social concern of various church leaders, to combat city slums and to ameliorate the conditions of the industrial worker, sought firmer realization and organizational embodiment.

Part of the idiom of the time was a boundless hope and confidence which found expression in church social welfare and institutional churches. As previously noted, one of the Federal Council's organizing mandates was to provide a vehicle for expressing what might be broadly termed the "social gospel." As the "official keeper" of the social gospel the Council gave it, perhaps for the first time, an official and recognized ecclesiastical form. Epitomizing its social interest, the Council adopted the declaration of the "Social Creed of the Churches" at its inception.

Many of the Social Creed's provisions were addressed to the dislocations arising from industrialization. Lest the churches lose their grip among the working classes, the social gospel served to express concern and to capture the allegiance of workers. According to John A. Hutchison:

Cooperation and federation were *forced* upon the churches by the

[9] In 1950, after forty-two years of existence, the Federal Council merged with seven other interdenominational functional agencies to form the National Council of the Churches of Christ in the United States of America.

[10] *We Are Not Divided* (New York: Round Table Press, 1941), p. 39.

strange new world of industry with its smoke and dirt, its poverty and strife into which America entered in the later years of the nineteenth century. . . . There emerged from this new situation a religious response which came to be termed the Social Gospel. . . . The Federal Council of Churches was born of the marriage of the ideas of church federation and the Social Gospel.[11]

In large measure, the Federal Council was a response to the social tasks which drew the churches together in common action. Unity of diverse denominations would best combat the social evils of the day. Providing the impetus for an application of the gospel to "every relation of human life" were the inequalities growing out of the social situation. The cause of church unity was championed by the churches' common reaction against the stirring injustices of society.

Perhaps an even more dramatic instance of social crisis as a source for stimulating church unity was the impact of World War I on the Federal Council of Churches. The Council girded itself in order to perform warborn tasks. In its early years, the Council lived a precarious existence. Then the war called for rapid expansion of its activities and unwittingly became a means of its unprecedented growth. War relief funds were collected for the stricken churches of Europe.[12] Personnel were added to man the important "General War-Time Commission of the Churches." In 1917, the Council initiated the Commission on Army and Navy Chaplains. Drawing extensively upon the churches, the federal government appealed to the nation's clergymen for help. Since the government found it obviously impossible to deal separately with numerous religious groups, the Federal Council of Churches became the logical centralized agency through which to function. Efforts of all the Protestant churches—with the exception of the pacifist groups—were coordinated through the Council.

[11] *Ibid.*, p. 99.

[12] Between 1915 and 1924, 1,500,000 dollars were dispensed to churches in Belgium and France. This sum seems slight in comparison to the 50,000,000 dollars handled by Church World Service during and immediately following World War II.

The Council "emerged from the war period as a vital and obviously permanent factor in the national consciousness," concluded Charles S. McFarland, one of its first executive secretaries.[13] In similar vein, Hutchison affirmed, "The Federal Council entered the war as a small, obscure organization, and it emerged as perhaps the most influential organization in American Protestantism, or indeed, in the entire American religious scene." [14] In times of emergency, the churches are most effective and can best be heard as a united body, rather than by the clamor of many discordant voices.

Observers of the current religious scene have frequently called attention to the lack of enthusiasm for social and political issues as a notable feature of our day in contrast to the 1930's. It would take us too far afield to analyze the issues involved in the contemporary decline of interest in the concerns which captured the imagination of social gospel leaders. Yet one cannot help but observe the kinship between the spirit of the older social gospel interest and the new interest in ecumenical affairs. The latter is imbued with a similar enthusiasm and passionate devotion to a just cause. Perhaps ecumenicity and social gospel interests go hand in hand. Among the earlier advocates of the ecumenical movement, the appeal for unity was frequently based on the plea that a divided church exerts a frail and ineffective influence in confronting the evils of the world and in redeeming the social order. As we shall frequently discover, one of the continuing strands in the drive toward church unity is the concerted effort of churchmen to make an effective impact upon the secular world. Common examination of critical social issues confronting the Church elicits a major thrust of unitive response. In short, the incentive for *social justice* provides an important contributing source of church unity on the American scene.[15]

[13] *Church Unity in Practice and Prophecy* (New York: The Macmillan Company, 1933), p. 66.
[14] *Op. cit.,* p. 175
[15] For a discussion of this point in relation to the World Council cf. Edward Duff, *The Social Thought of the World Council of Churches* (London: Long-

Formation of the Federal Council marks a significant point of departure in the developing church unity movement. Moreover, it was to have far-reaching importance both at home and abroad. Accordingly, William Adams Brown, a pioneer ecumenical leader, noted:

It is difficult to exaggerate the importance of the contribution to Christian unity which was made by the formation and development of the Federal Council. It was not only the public recognition of the fact that the unity movement, long a foster child of the Churches, had now been finally adopted as a regular member of the family. It not only committed the Churches as such to the seeking of a more just and brotherly society, but by its adoption of the federal principle, as a method of organization appropriate to the genius of the American Churches, a precedent was set which was destined to be followed thirty years later in the creation of the World Council.[16]

This development of the Federal Council was symptomatic of broader and deeper trends toward unity in the life of the churches which were developing during the same period of time: (1) organic mergers involving denominations, (2) the conciliar movement, (3) local community centered churches, and (4) the practice of comity.[17] Each was influenced by the experience of the Federal Council and, in turn, had an influence on its experience. This was particularly true of the conciliar

---

mans, Green and Company, 1956). The "Life and Work Movement" has partly been a vehicle for expressing social concern, particularly through the Oxford (1937) and Amsterdam (1948) Conferences. At Amsterdam the concept "Responsible Society" was voiced, and given fuller articulation at the Evanston Assembly (1954).

[16] *Toward a United Church* (New York: Charles Scribner's Sons, 1946), p. 51.

[17] Other signs of unity which will not be detailed include: (1) Six major proposals for multiple denominational mergers advocated since 1918. The latest of these proposals, known as "The Greenwich Plan," is still pending. Perhaps the most widely known proposal among laymen is the so-called "E. Stanley Jones Plan." (2) Developments on the college campus, particularly the unprecedented growth of the ecumenically-minded college chaplaincy, and the formation of the Campus Christian Fellowship which merges the student movements of the United Church of Christ, Disciples of Christ, Evangelical United Brethren, and the United Presbyterian Church. (3) The widespread sharing of hymns and hymn tunes, revealing a process of ever-growing convergence in church music. (4) The sharing of religious education curriculum materials across denominational lines.

movement, and it will be necessary to discuss the Federal Council and its successor organization the National Council again when the growth of church councils is considered. So basic was the Federal Council to the emerging church unity of this century, however, that it has deserved special consideration here.

Meanwhile, the emergence of a "common-core Protestantism" should be noted as a second great sign of growing church unity.

II. EMERGENCE OF A "COMMON-CORE PROTESTANTISM"

Closer harmony in thought and practice, and a liberal sharing among the major groups of American Protestantism, has been increasingly apparent.

A typical example which leaps to the eye is the pervasive tendency for Protestant churches to adopt similar design and furnishings in their sanctuaries—the widespread use of the cross and divided chancel, and the transformation of the communion table into an altar.

Widely-shared, definable, common characteristics gave rise to what might be called a common core Protestantism—a faith and practice, which evolved not as the exclusive province of any single group.[18] Its ascendancy signifies the erosion of Protestant particularity. Of course, one finds it difficult to distinguish clearly between cause and effect, to know whether the common-core stimulates further forms of unity, or whether it flows from the unity already realized. That a wide sharing among Protestant groups exists is undeniable.

This section of our study seeks (1) to document the components of a common-core Protestantism by considering five selected indices: doctrinal consensus, interchangeable member-

---

[18] Cf. Douglas Horton, "Now the United Church of Christ," *Christian Century* (June 12, 1957), 733: According to Horton, "Ninety percent of the procedures of any denomination today are untainted by denominational association. There is nothing especially Congregational about an every-member canvass for funds, nothing downright Presbyterian about a church choir." Horton's estimation might be a bit high, but it does recognize the existence of a common-core Protestantism.

ship, interchangeable ministry, organizational structure, and common ethos; (2) to identify the social bases and indicate the tendencies for common-core Protestantism to reflect the underlying unity of a common-core American culture.[19]

A. DOCTRINAL CONSENSUS. One important index of a common-core Protestantism is doctrinal consensus—a broad sharing of faith in basic convictions. Of course, vigorous theological debates remain, and often the price paid for consensus is silence, so that disagreements fail to come to the fore. Moreover, doctrinal consensus may issue from ill-defined and ambiguous meanings which generate lip service concurrence. The main point, however, remains this: disagreements do not typically follow along denominational lines. As frequently pointed out, differences within denominations are equally as sharp— if not sharper—than those between them.[20] Try to find a distinctive Congregational, Methodist, or Presbyterian doctrine of Christ. Doctrinal differences separating Protestants today do not correspond to the lines of contemporary denominations, but tend to cut across these boundaries.

In preparation for the Oberlin Conference on Faith and Order, the Minneapolis Study Group on Doctrinal Consensus and Conflict circulated a check-list questionnaire to five thousand respondents. Results of the survey indicate a kind of "theological ecumenicity" with considerable agreement on the nature of the Church, the ground of salvation, the Person of Christ,

---

[19] While the evidence for a common-core Protestantism may be gathered fairly easily by a search of the literature, there is little material that is addressed to the question of *why*, or what its social bases might be. In the absence of tested hypotheses, our analysis of the social bases must perforce be speculative and presented as tentative findings rather than assured conclusions.

[20] This is a finding of the Commission on the "Church's Unity in Life and Worship." Cf. Willard Sperry, "The Non-Theological Factors in the Making and Unmaking of Church Union" (Geneva: Faith and Order Paper No. 84, 1937). Our index of theological consensus here being discussed is obviously not with reference to the debates among various schools of theology; it is rather from the church public's assimilation of the faith. Whether there is growing consensus among contemporary theologians in America is a moot point.

and the sacrament of the Lord's Supper.[21] Here is an apt summation of the implications of the Minneapolis Study Group's statistical findings:

On the four theological areas surveyed, all the respondents could be included in the Methodist Church without increasing the diversity which is already represented by the Methodist clergy. 94% could join the Lutheran or Presbyterian Churches without increasing the diversity in the views of the Bible which already exist in the clergy of these denominations. . . . 72% could be Episcopalian or Lutheran on the doctrine of the sacrament of baptism, and more than 95% could be Presbyterians. Four or five possible positions on the Lord's Supper are taken by Episcopal clergy, and these account for 96.4% of the total responses.[22]

This relatively high incidence of theological consensus minimizes one particular source of potential conflict, and enables common identification and greater mutuality among various religious groups.

Are there underlying social conditions which contribute to the current theological consensus? Our present state of knowledge permits us only to speculate on answers to this question. Therefore the following social bases are offered tentatively as suggestive areas for further exploration.

1. *Common exposure.* Common exposure tends to further theological consensus. Our earlier discussion of cultural unity noted that common exposure likely affords a "permeable character" to American society. This is relevant to the development of theological consensus, as distinctive theological views—sustained by sectional, ethnic, class, or racial bases—are permeated by a similar theological frame of reference. Such exposure is made possible by free and widespread population mobility, mass reading clubs for theological and religious books, and interaction with other viewpoints of a religious and secular nature.

[21] Reported by Walter G. Muelder, "Institutionalism in Relation to Unity and Disunity," *The Nature of the Unity We Seek,* ed. Paul S. Minear (St. Louis: The Bethany Press, 1958), p. 92.
[22] *Ibid.*

2. Accommodation of church to society. As church membership expands rapidly and joining a church becomes a popularly accepted social pattern, stress on doctrines becomes less pronounced. Where the church enjoys a harmonious relationship and close identification with the society, less compelling reasons exist for doctrinal articulation and distinctiveness. When religious values merge more with social values, it becomes difficult to distinguish one from the other. With increased sharing of nonreligious goals and norms, allegiances to distinctive religious doctrines diminish in intensity. Theological content assumes more vague and indefinite rather than more specific and precise meaning. Just as cultural values and symbols of national unity take on a generalized content, so also theological doctrines assume a diffused meaning, and become "all things to all men" to which all may subscribe.

3. Changing church practices and techniques. In practice the church places less stress on denominational distinctiveness. This trend is discernible in many areas. As standards for church membership become inclusive, correct doctrine is no longer the test for membership. Nowadays, rarely does a denomination convince a person to join on the grounds that it alone bears the true doctrines; the claim to be the true Church is relegated to the limbo of arrogancy. Organized activities in churches tend to follow along interest-group lines; they are underdeveloped in areas of theological discipline and discussion. As the church performs more diverse functions and seeks a more inclusive membership, less emphasis is placed on indoctrination and inculcation of distinctive denominational teachings, tending thereby to minimize and obscure theological differences.

B. INTERCHANGEABLE MEMBERSHIP. Another mark of common-core Protestantism is the free movement from denomination to denomination, or the seemingly interchangeable membership of the laity. While such practice is commonly acknowledged, studies are few and far between. Suggestive data may be gleaned from various church membership studies and from preferences revealed in church and community surveys. One such study shows the free flow of membership in the ninety-two new Congregational-Christian churches aided by the denomination's Board of Home Missions between 1944 and 1955.[23] The study reports that in the combined membership of over 28,000, only 25 per cent were formerly affiliated with Congregational-Christian Churches. Seventy-five per cent of the members of new Congregational-Christian Churches come from a diversity of other denominations. A Protestant Council Survey of a Congregational church in the south Bronx finds that only 5 per cent of the current members claim a Congregational background. Ninety-five per cent represent either none or a variety of previous religious affiliations.

Available evidence indicates that denominational "passing" is commonplace and done with relative ease. Sometimes curious church partners result from the reshuffling of members. In one case, a Missouri Synod Lutheran Church in Illinois has as its lay president a former Southern Baptist. Denominational differences to the lay mind seem to be eroding. There has come into the open what may be called a "lay doctrine of equivalence," which shows signs of impatience with strict denominational ties.

How might the social bases of membership interchangeability be interpreted? Again, we may here offer some speculative answers:

1. Segmental participation. Our earlier discussion of the organizational revolution noted the tendency for individuals to broaden their organizational loyalties. The quality of participation in organizations tends to be partial, so that the individual depends less upon any one organization. One participates in a whole host of voluntary associations, but his involvement is segmental. One tends to avoid intensive organizational commitment. Doubtless, the relatively easy transition from one denomination to another is enhanced by the lack of strong attach-

[23] Yoshio Fukuyama, *New Churches Aided by Board of Home Missions* (New York: Congregational-Christian Churches, 1957), p. 4.

ments to any particular denomination—a tendency reflecting the segmental participation of a mass society.

2. Population mobility. The migration and redistribution of a large segment of the population—a process to be detailed in a later context—provides the occasion for developing new patterns of religious affiliation. Mobility often disrupts older patterns and accepted ways and exposes the individual to new experiences and contacts with people from diverse religious backgrounds. In a new community to which one moves, one's former denomination may not be present.

3. Lay values. In the scale of lay values, such items as a "friendly minister," "convenient neighborhood location," or "good Sunday school for the kids" hold greater priority than preference for a particular denominational allegiance. These standards of choice have a levelling effect upon denominations in the mind of the laity and tend to encourage interchangeable membership.

4. Institutional standards of success. Since institutional success is largely interpreted by size and accession of members, not a few Protestant ministers seek to "make a good showing" in their annual reports to denominational headquarters. With such a motivation, differences are minimized and membership made attractive to the largest possible number. While minimizing denominational or doctrinal stands, appeals are frequently based on "good fellowship in our church," "people whom you like and will like you," "well-rounded program of activities." The commonplace program of "fellowship evangelism," which sends out lay people to evangelize, often means that laymen seek out others of similar social and economic standing; or invitations are based on friendliness rather than on denominational or doctrinal grounds. In order to conform to standards of institutional success, an eagerness to attract those of varying denominational backgrounds encourages interchangeability of membership.

5. Intermarriage. Intermarriage across denominational lines contributes to the free movement of church membership. In many instances marriage partners of different backgrounds transfer to the church of one of the spouses or choose a mutually acceptable third affiliation. Although studies on the frequency of marriage across denominational lines are precious few, one such inquiry of the United Lutheran Church in America yields significant data. It reports that 58 per cent of the Lutherans studied in 382 congregations found their mates outside of the Lutheran Church. Three fifths married members of other Protestant denominations.[24]

6. Social status. Some students of community life, such as Lloyd Warner, suggest that changing denominations is a vehicle of upward social mobility.[25] Hence one may move from the Nazarenes, to the Baptist, to the Methodist, thence to the Presbyterian or Congregational Church in a fashion not unlike an ascending staircase. In the Lutheran study of mixed marriages cited above, the authors find that "the lower the status of the Lutheran Church the higher the percentage of members marrying outside of the church, with a relatively large proportion . . . women who marry in an upward direction." [26]

The high degree of interchangeability of church members suggests that denominational loyalties are becoming secondary. Such erosion of allegiances and modification of loyalties provide fertile soil for the growth and development of church unity movements in the United States.

C. INTERCHANGEABLE MINISTRY. As with church members, likewise considerable mobility occurs among the clergy, pointing to the existence of an interchangeable ministry. The movement of clergy back and forth across denominational lines is commonplace knowledge, but seldom documented by research.

H. Paul Douglass notes that in 1930 the Congregational Churches ordained ninety-six men, but accepted ninety-two

[24] James H. S. Bossard and Eleanor S. Boll, *One Marriage, Two Faiths* (New York: The Ronald Press, 1957) , p. 56.
[25] *Democracy in Jonesville* (New York: Harper & Brothers, 1949) , pp. 153 ff. It happens that in Jonesville, the Federated Church enjoys the highest social status.
[26] Bossard and Boll, *op. cit.,* pp. 57 ff.

more ordained by other denominations.[27] Similarly, in 1926 the General Assembly of the Presbyterian Church, U.S.A. reported that 38 per cent of all its accessions to the ministry during the previous five years had come from other denominations. More recently, from 1951 to 1955, the Presbyterian Church, U.S.A. received 372 ministers from other denominations, while losing 209 to other church bodies.

A recent study of the situation in the Congregational Christian Churches checked a five-year period from 1950 to 1954, and concluded:

> During *each* of these last five years we have received an average of 221 new ministers into Congregational Christian standing as ordained ministers. Of these, 133 have been ordained in our own churches and 88 have come by transfer of ministerial standing from other denominations.[28]

Between 1950 and 1954, 40 per cent of the ministers joining the Congregational Christian fold came from other denominations. These recruits came from forty-two different religious groups, with the larger numbers transferring from Baptist, Methodist, Presbyterian, Disciples of Christ, Evangelical and Reformed, and Evangelical United Brethren backgrounds—in the order as listed.

A careful study of Yale University Divinity School students in 1954 with respect to their patterns of denominational change indicates that from one fourth to one fifth of the student body made a change in denomination or planned to make such a change during college or seminary study. There is some evidence that students who change denominations during their course of study at Yale tend to elect the Presbyterian and Episcopal churches.[29]

[27] H. Paul Douglass, "Ecumenicity in America," in *Toward World-Wide Christianity*, ed., O. F. Nolde (New York: Harper & Brothers, 1946), p. 179.
[28] Fred S. Buschmeyer, "Our Ministry: Some Facts and Figures," *Advance*, 147 (October, 19, 1955), p. 12.
[29] W. J. Warren and R. L. Powers, "A Study of Denominational Changes Made by Students at Yale Divinity School" (New Haven: Social Ethics Library, 1954), pp. 8 ff.

What social factors encourage denominational mobility among the clergy? At the outset, let us recognize that changing denominations—like vocational changes in other fields—is usually a highly personal affair, involving diverse motives which cannot be sorted out easily. In addition, "one man's meat may be another's poison." To cite an example, one clergyman decided to change to The Methodist Church because he liked the security offered by a system of guaranteed job placement through a Methodist Conference; on the other hand, another minister left the same denomination because the transfer from parish to parish, with the consequent uprootedness in family life and the severing of community ties, made him insecure. Despite individual preferences involved in changing ministries, however, one can still identify some general social considerations.

1. Relieving institutional strain. Changing one's denomination offers a means for relieving institutional strain. In a situation of conflict (between a minister and some particular aspect of his denomination's life, practice, or thought) tension may be alleviated by altering the denominational context. Examples of institutional strain are manifested either in the desire for a more structured framework and fixed tradition, or in the felt need for greater freedom and autonomy; in the dissatisfaction with a group's doctrinal stand, or moralistic orientation (e.g., smoking and drinking injunctions) ; or its lack of a sufficiently liberal social and political outlook. Thus change of one's ministry may result from the effort to relieve strain.[30]

2. Shortage of ministerial supply. Changing denominations would be virtually impossible, if a receptive attitude on the part of most denominational executives were absent. Such openness makes denominational shifts a live option. That religious groups express an eagerness to receive ordained clergymen from other bodies at least partially reflects the shortage of trained ministers to fulfill growing denominational demands. Such deficiency encourages a kind of "competitive bidding" among the de-

---

[30] For an analysis of conflict as one source of social change, as developed at fuller length cf. Merton. *op. cit.*

nominations in the recruitment of ministerial supply. Hence, interchangeable ministry is favored not only by an individual's readiness for change across denominational lines, but by a denomination's eagerness to accept those desiring to change and by the ease of mobility itself.

3. *Common exposure.* Interchangeable ministry is facilitated to a large extent by common exposure—a general similarity of background and outlook, growing out of interpersonal contacts and shared, common experiences. The "social distance" between clergymen of different denominations lessens through the practice of drawing from the same reservoir of theological books and journals. Such common exposure tends to promote a community of similar theological thought and discourse. In this connection, the role of leading Protestant theological seminaries which are undenominational in character bears examination. A study might well compare the rate of change for ministers educated in denominational colleges and seminaries with those trained in a non-sectarian college and an interdenominational seminary. Common exposure and personal contacts across denominational lines may well serve as a "triggering" device for changing denominations. At least it is conducive to a common-core Protestantism.

4. *Vocational goals.* Earlier we reviewed the trend toward specialization in a technological society. Similar developments increasingly affect the ministry as a profession. Multiple church staffs with specialized ministries are commonplace. Frequently a person trains or does graduate study for a specialized ministry, such as inner city work; pastoral counselling; religious research; church social work; industrial, hospital, prison, or other institutional chaplaincy. Since denominations proceed at a different pace in their development of fields for specialized ministries, a person may change to the denomination which offers the best opportunities for his specialized services in order to fulfill his vocational goal. Or, an individual trained for specialized service may choose a particular position regardless of denominational sponsorship, and later transfer his ministerial connection.

5. Status goal. Doubtless some degree of mobility springs from status aspirations, as one seeks to identify with a denomination which, in one's mind, enjoys high social status. While the status goal is more hidden than revealed, it has some support from evidence earlier reported and from the impression that Episcopalians, Congregationalists and Presbyterians stand out high in gaining recruits from other denominations. Conversely such groups as Southern Baptists, American Baptists, Methodists, and Disciples might be expected to relinquish a considerable flock of their clergy via the migration process. In turn, these groups may draw from those lower in the status hierarchy.

Many other social factors are involved in the pattern of interchangeable ministry. A few might be mentioned—such as preference for a certain geographical setting to perform one's ministry—for example, California or New England—the lessening of doctrinal distinctiveness, opportunity for job advancement, higher salaries and perquisites, or the choice of ministers by lay pulpit committees without regard necessarily for denominational ties. Interchangeable ministry constitutes an index of common-core Protestantism, which underlies the movement of organized church unity.

D. ORGANIZATIONAL STRUCTURE. In the realm of organizational structure, there is traditional acknowledgment of three forms of church government—Episcopalian, Presbyterian, and Congregational. Yet one notes with surprise a growing similarity among these three forms. Walter Rauschenbusch, prophetic leader of the Social Gospel movement, was perhaps speaking more prophetically than he realized when he said:

The divergent types of church government which separated these bodies (Methodist, Baptist, Presbyterian, Disciples, Congregationalists, German, and Dutch Reformed), have been worn down by generations of practical experience, and they have gravitated toward the same methods of work and life. The Presbyterian type has become more congregational, and the Congregational type has become more presbyterian and representative. . . . The most decisive fact for the essential unity of these great bodies is that they have all thoroughly assimilated the principle of democracy and are allowing any *jure divino* theories to fall into oblivion.[31]

In preparation for the Oberlin Conference on Faith and Order, the New York Study Group came to the arresting conclusion that church governments—whether episcopal, presbyterian, or congregational in form—are similar in function and power structure. "Theories and practices of church government, which to an external view seem widely divergent and even divisive, disclose, to a more interior examination, many striking correspondences and similarities." [32] Indeed, the organizational channels for meeting responsibilities and functions blend so much that the study group reports a large area of agreement and essential unity in governmental, organizational, and administrative matters. Yet these similarities of administrative authority and practice are often obscured by different terminology and titles. For example, the authority of an "executive secretary" in a congregational polity is similar to—if not greater than—the power wielded by an administrative head in an episcopal structure.

What role have social factors played in the convergence of the different polities toward a common form?

1. Democratic context. Religious organizations have developed in the context of democratic political institutions which reserve a responsible role for lay leadership and broad participation. Our nation was founded free of established clerical hierarchy. Hence ecclesiastical authority increasingly rests upon voluntary consent and support by its constituency. The prominence of lay leadership in the life of American churches leads to democratization of religious organizations.

2. Organizational revolution. In view of the organizational

---

[31] Quoted by Archer Bass, *Protestantism in the United States* (New York: Thomas Y. Crowell Company, 1929), p. 275.

[32] New York Study Group, "Report on Authority and Freedom in Church Government," North American Conference on Faith and Order, Orientation Paper, Section 7, p. 1.

revolution (earlier discussed) and the need for functional co-ordination, each of the major denominations has had to elaborate a complex national administrative machinery based upon agencies, committees, and boards. These organizational structures are patterned after secular large-scale organizations and inevitably assume similar behavior patterns, guided by standards of efficient performance of functions.[33] To state the matter as a sociological axiom: common functions tend to produce common structures. Hence the organizational lives of the three forms of church government have tended to become more alike as they confront similar large-scale responsibilities.

E. COMMON ETHOS. Less well-defined as an area of similarity is the common ethos pervading American Protestantism. Certain characteristic elements stand out in contrast to European or Asian forms of Christianity.[34] Yet, as in our earlier discussion of value themes, the components of a common ethos of American Protestantism appear somewhat vague. In part, this is so because we deal here with a more elusive and subtle subject than the other items in our accounting of common-core Protestantism.

More significantly, however, so inextricably intertwined with the rest of American culture has the common religious ethos become, that it is difficult to separate the one from the other. For example, European commentators have noted the activism of American religious life. The roots of activism are many, but certainly two sources stand out. On the one hand, pioneer life

[33] A number of Protestant denominations, including the Southern and American Baptists and the Methodists, have been recently studied by management consultants in terms of their efficiency rating.

[34] An "indigenous American faith" is discerned by many observers of the religious scene. Cf. Ronald Osborn, *The Spirit of American Christianity* (New York: Harper & Brothers, 1958); Jerald C. Brauer, *Protestantism in America* (Philadelphia: The Westminster Press, 1953); and Bilheimer, *op. cit.*, pp. 25-52. In an address to the General Board of the National Council of Churches, H. Richard Niebuhr discusses the emergence of an "American Church" and notes the coincidence between the economic system and the "religious system" in America. Cf. "American Church Seen as a Reality," *New York Times,* October 7, 1955. Also cf. Willard L. Sperry, *Religion in America* (New York: The Macmillan Company, 1946), *passim.*

and modern urban industrialism foster an activism toward the environment; on the other hand, the influence of the early Puritans and the work ethic of Calvinism with its activist conception of God also encourage an "intense promotion of laborious and dutiful living." [35] Recognizing this web of religious and cultural interrelatedness, we intend to limit our discussion in this section to a listing of traits which form some of the ingredients of a common ethos.[36]

1. An activism which appears in various phases of church life —the evangelistic spreading of the gospel, the drives for membership, finance, and expansion, the innumerable church committees and laymen's activities—confirming what De Tocqueville called the "strange unrest of Americans."

2. The prominence of the minister as a personality as over against his office; parishioners tend to identify with the minister, so that membership in a particular church, frequently hinges on the minister's popularity. Churches are familiarly referred to by the preacher's name rather than by the denominational or the given church name.

3. The emphasis on fellowship and friendship in the church, with churches featuring a considerable program of social and recreational activities, such as potluck suppers, dances, picnics, and "coffee hours." Not a few churches announce on their public bulletin boards such notices as, "This is a friendly church," "A place to meet friends and to worship," "A friendly fellowship awaits you," or "Fellowship suppers at the friendly church." An expression of this tendency comes in the assumption shared by many Protestants that an "unfriendly church is not a Christian church."

4. The responsible role played by laymen in church activities —as officers, fund raisers, callers, teachers, scout leaders. Many churches feature countless committees and programs for the sake of "involving" as many laymen as possible in leadership posts.

[35] Niebuhr, *Social Sources of Denominationalism,* p. 203.
[36] Osborn, *op. cit.* Many of these characteristics are suggested by Osborn; they are admittedly broad generalizations and subject to discussion.

Sometimes these positions are viewed as a way to gain status and recognition.

5. The concern for humanitarian goals and human welfare, exemplified in seasonal giving of food, clothing, and money for home and foreign missions and for relief. American Protestantism has largely institutionalized the concern for social justice, as social action and education agencies with professional staff are found in nearly every major denomination; not a few local churches have standing committees to deal with social issues.

6. The search for a simple faith, which is concrete and pragmatic in temperament, tending to distrust theological discussions or to regard them with diffidence and disdain. Hence the popular appeal of an evangelist who can state the faith in simple, unambiguous terms.[37]

7. The emphasis on an educated clergy, with the clergyman frequently doubling as schoolteacher in the early days. American church historian William Warren Sweet has observed that less than one hundred years ago New Englanders regarded Baptists and Methodists as outcastes.[38] Their preachers were noted for their "bad grammar, low idioms, and the euphony of a nasal twang in preaching." [39] Obviously this cultural and educational gulf has been bridged, since such marked external social differences no longer appear prominent among Baptists and Methodists.

The common ethos pervading American Protestantsism and centering on such characteristics as activism, personality, friendship, humanitarian concern, voluntarism, pragmatic temperament, and education should recall to mind our earlier discussion of the value themes of American culture. Values sustaining a common ethos have affinities to the values of a common-core American culture. Likely a "strain toward consistency" operates among the institutions of society, as these cultural values are im-

[37] A recent book which perhaps symbolizes American religious practicality—or a corruption thereof—is called *Pray Your Weight Away!*

[38] *American Culture and Religion* (Dallas: Southern Methodist University Press, 1951), p. 108.

[39] *Ibid.*

ported into the life and work of the church. In turn the church reinforces and, in some cases, has spawned and given its blessings to cultural values. Laymen serve as carriers of values from institution to institution. Of course, clergymen are also effective mediators of cultural values. In this connection, the role of personal and institutional success and efficiency will be elaborated in subsequent chapters.

In drawing to a close our discussion of common-core Protestantism, let us again stress that the various components and their social bases are related in dynamic interaction. Separated only for purposes of analysis, they are woven into the warp and woof of American Protestantism. Their sharing in faith and practice in ever-widening circles contributes to the ascendancy of church unity in American Protestantism.

III. SUMMARY

In summary, developments in the church unity movement in the United States have heightened since the twentieth century, although earlier ripples in this direction are discernible. The turning of the tide is characterized by rising currents of co-operation and collaboration, and the ebb of proliferation and partition.

The founding of the Federal Council of Churches in 1908 was a highly significant landmark. In answer to the question why this particular movement for unity reached its consummation when so many others had failed, we noted the contribution of social and cultural factors—particularly the problems of urbanization and industrialization, the Social Gospel concerns, and the impetus of World War I.

Partly a quest for greater unity and partly an achievement of that quest is the development of a common-core Protestantism, which tends to reflect the common-core culture. Some of its major earmarks were suggested—doctrinal consensus, interchangeable membership, interchangeable ministry, organizational structure, and common ethos. Each of these components

interacts with broader changes taking place in the social structure, and to a significant degree, is dependent upon these social
changes. The growing recognition of a common-core Protestantism, of a sharing of religious life and thought across denominational boundaries, furnishes much of the ground for the
drive toward church unity. A fitting conclusion to our discussion
of common-core Protestantism comes from a National Council
document which maintains that American church unity is

grounded in a great central core of Christian conviction held in
common by the co-operating denominations that reveals an identifiable common mind. Although American communions have a varied
heritage of Christian faith and practice, there has emerged a common spirit of sharing that is a model of the democratic ideal and
temper of American life. This common spirit has enabled the
churches to unite in their effort to create a Christian land governed
by Christian principles.[40]

In the next four chapters the examination of organizational
forms, which are both signs and instrumentalities of church
unity in the United States, will claim our attention. Our first
area of analysis concerns organic mergers and reunions of once
separated groups.

[40] *Criteria for Self Evaluation and Measurement* (New York: Office of Councils of Churches, National Council of Churches, 1955), p. 7.

4. Denominational Mergers and Reunions

I. INTRODUCTION

Successful mergers within denominational families and between communions, as well as conversations with a view to organic merger, are involving more and more Protestant groups. Although many regard these mergers and reunions as the most authentic expression of church-unity, others view them as relatively insignificant, on the grounds that the parties to the union were needlessly divided in the first place. The important point to ponder, however, is that organic mergers are now a fact, whereas previously they were practically nonexistent. Between 1870—when the Old School and the New School Presbyterians reunited—and 1905, not a single instance of church union is recorded in the United States.[41]

Since 1905, no less than eleven organic mergers within the same denominational family and four unions across denominational lines have been consummated.[42] These unions have reduced the number of major Protestant groups from thirty-four to fifteen. Moreover, various merger discussions now pending include at least thirty parties. The May, 1959, proposal by the United Presbyterian Church invited nine sister bodies related to the Reformed tradition to join it in seeking organic unity.

[41] Samuel McCrea Cavert, "Christian Unity in America," *The Church Through Half a Century*, ed. Samuel McCrea Cavert and H. P. Van Dusen (New York: Charles Scribner's Sons, 1936), p. 360.

[42] Excluded from this counting are countless consolations of smaller groups and synods. Also excluded are mergers like the Pillar Fire with the Fire Baptized Holiness Church. Indeed, since 1911, fourteen Pentecostal groups have merged into five bodies for a combined membership of 556,000.

Several of the pending proposals give real promise of being added to the list of completed organic unions.

A listing of the successful organic mergers of the present century includes the following: [43]

Intra-Denominational Type

1906 Presbyterian Church, U.S.A. and Cumberland Presbyterian Church became Presbyterian Church, U.S.A.

1911 Northern Baptist Convention and Free Baptist Churches became American Baptist Convention.

1917 Hauge's Norwegian Evangelical Lutheran Synod and Synod of the Norwegian Evangelical Church of America and the United Lutheran Church in America became Norwegian Church of America. The name changed to Evangelical Lutheran Church.

1918 General Synod of the Lutheran Church in the United States and General Council of the Lutheran Church in the United States and United Synod of the South became United Lutheran Church.

1920 Presbyterian Church, U.S.A. and Welsh Calvinist Methodist Church became Presbyterian Church, U.S.A.

1922 Evangelical Association and United Evangelical Church became Evangelical Church.

1924 Reformed Church in the United States and Hungarian Reformed Church in America became Reformed Church in the United States.

1930 Lutheran Synod of Buffalo, Evangelical Lutheran Synod of Iowa and Other States, and Evangelical Joint Synod of Ohio and Other States became American Lutheran Church.

1939 Methodist Episcopal Church, Methodist Episcopal Church,

[43] Another form of organic merger, known as intercommunion, or the recognition of one another's sacraments, was achieved between the Protestant Episcopal and the Polish National Catholic Churches in 1946. Excluded from our discussion also are various forms of co-operation across denominational lines, a good example being the Baptist Joint Committee on Public Affairs—a venture bridging racial and sectional differences, since Negro and Southern groups are involved. The Joint Committee combines the efforts of various Baptist groups to advance the cause of religious liberty. Included are such groups as Southern Baptist Convention, National Baptist Convention, U.S.A., Inc., Baptist General Conference of America, North American Baptist General Conference, et cetera.

South, and Methodist Protestant Church became The Methodist Church.

1946 Evangelical Church and Church of the United Brethren in Christ became Evangelical United Brethren Church.

1958 Presbyterian Church, U.S.A. and United Presbyterian Church of North America became United Presbyterian Church in the U.S.A.

Trans-Denominational Type

1925 Congregational Churches and Evangelical Protestant Churches of North America became Congregational Churches (German Congregational Church also affiliating).

1931 Congregational Churches and Christian Churches became Congregational-Christian Churches.

1934 Reformed Church in the United States and Evangelical Synod of North America became Evangelical and Reformed Church.

1957 Congregational-Christian Churches and Evangelical and Reformed Church became United Church of Christ.

II. ROLE OF SOCIAL FACTORS

Behind all these mergers and reunions, sometimes lurking in the background and other times prominent in the foreground, social factors operate. Of course, they are not the sole considerations; nor are they absent from the unsuccessful merger efforts.

At least a dozen proposals have been terminated or abandoned. These reasons are cited for their failure: one of the parties became involved in another negotiation; strong personalities feared they might lose their leadership status; smaller groups feared they would be "swallowed up" by merger with a larger denomination; while top leaders enjoyed friendly contacts, the rank-and-file members lacked sufficient contacts with their counterparts; stubborn resistance to change; and residual institutional problems, such as handling real estate, properties, pension funds, and debts.

In treating the extensive denominational mergers and reunions, this chapter can merely list the social factors which are influential, and then cite a few examples from the experience of consummated unions. Since the full story of these mergers is too complex for complete coverage, two case studies presented in fuller detail will illustrate the factors involved: the mergers within Lutheranism, reflecting the so-called "intra-denominational" type, and the union between the Congregational-Christian and Evangelical and Reformed, representing the "trans-denominational" type.

1. Sectional changes. Church groups which originated under frontier conditions or began as regional bodies outgrew these confining ties with the shrivelling of the frontier and the erosion of sectional allegiance. Thus the earliest merger of the present century became possible when the Cumberland Presbyterian Church recognized that the frontier life which largely accounted for its birth no longer existed. Similarly, the way for reunion was paved when the Free Baptist Churches, centered in New England, grew out of their regional boundaries. Instead of sectionally isolated groups, wider and more complementary geographical distribution was sought, as in the case of the Congregational and Christian Churches whose union spanned sectional differences.

2. Ethnic changes. As immigrant churches shed their foreign features—which furnished the foundation for many denominations—and form common ties to American culture, the way for merger is open. This Americanization process is involved, at least as a contributing factor, in a number of cases, notably the Welsh Calvinist Methodist and the Presbyterian Church, U.S.A.; Evangelical Association and United Evangelical Church; Congregational Churches and Evangelical Protestants; and the several mergers involving Lutheran bodies. Typical is the experience of the two parties to the Evangelical and Reformed merger. Formerly called German Evangelical Synod of North America and German Reformed Church, both groups dropped the ethnic label and came to use the English language in the process of Americanization. According to Carl E.

103

Schneider, the German Evangelical Synod was "put to the task of emancipating itself from the ties which bound it to the fatherland, and establishing such contacts with the new environment as would constitute it an American body." [44] In the case of The Methodist Church, which was rent into a Northern and Southern division and united in 1939, the split was mainly, though not exclusively, over the slavery issue. With the lessening of hostilities and the healing of old wounds, the original cause for schism began to subside.

3. *Class changes.* Similarity in social class status or increased socio-economic affinity as groups ascend in class standing, in part, encourages denominational mergers. Thus in the instance of the Free Baptists, previously cited, this appeal is mentioned as an argument for union. "The two peoples are of the same quality. Neither is aristocratic. Both denominations are composed of the great, solid, sensible, middle class, with an inclusiveness which reaches to either extreme." [45] In the merger forming the Evangelical United Brethren, Paul H. Eller, church historian of the group, aptly noted:

If the fathers belonged to the religiously neglected poor, their sons were neither religiously neglected nor poor. If the fathers were dissatisfied with a middle class complacency, their sons were prone to be quite satisfied with it.[46]

In the negotiations between the Protestant Episcopal and Presbyterian U.S.A. Churches, which failed to bear fruit, Charles Kean reminded us that a frequent argument advanced in favor of union asserted that both groups draw their members from the same social class. As Kean put it, "Cultural similarities between average Episcopalian and Presbyterian congregations

[44] "The Origin of the German Evangelical Synod of North America" (unpublished Ph.D. dissertation, University of Chicago, 1935), p. 3.

[45] *Two Denominations Uniting* (New York: Special Committee of Cooperation and Union of Baptists and Free Baptists, 1913), pp. 12-13.

[46] *These Evangelical United Brethren* (Dayton, Ohio: Otterbein Press, 1950), p. 91.

seemed to outweigh in importance the differences in religious tradition." [47]

4. Drives toward institutional strength. In view of the organizational revolution characterizing present-day society, and in order to exercise significant power, the pressure toward centralization and organizational co-ordination operates as a contributing source of organic merger. As with organized bureaucracies in other areas of life, so churches too are caught up in the inherent logic of established boards and agencies to expand in outreach, to solidify their gains, to multiply their functions, and to perpetuate themselves. In addition, the increasing demand for technical services calls for specialized and technically trained personnel, for which the supply is hardly adequate. Such organizational pressures often function covertly, but remain a reality underlying many mergers.

III. CASE STUDIES

The role of social factors will be seen more clearly in a more extensive treatment of two concrete cases. The first one actually involves three consummated unions among Lutherans, which will be considered chronologically, taking up the first two together.

A. LUTHERAN MERGERS. The first of the Lutheran mergers in the present century included the Hauge's Norwegian Evangelical Lutheran Synod, the Synod of the Norwegian Evangelical Church of America, and the United Norwegian Lutheran Church in America. These three formed the Norwegian Church of America in 1917. By 1946 the united group discarded its ethnic label and assumed the name Evangelical Lutheran Church.

One year later, in 1918, the General Synod of the Lutheran Church in the United States, the General Council of the Lutheran Church in the United States, and the United Synod

[47] *The Road to Reunion* (Greenwich: The Seabury Press, 1958), p. 20.

of the South joined forces in creating the United Lutheran Church.

As a result of the earlier union, the Norwegian Church of America became the largest Scandinavian group. With its 961,000 members, it ranks today as the third largest Lutheran body in America.

The formation of the United Lutheran Church brought into being the largest single organization of Lutherans in the nation. Sometimes dubbed the "most American" of the various Lutheran groups, the United Lutheran Church repeatedly shows signs of adaptability and openness in spirit and in thought.[48] Publicly, it announced a policy desiring merger "with any or all" Lutheran groups in America. Having held "consultative membership" in the Federal Council, United Lutherans hold full membership in the National Council and assume an active leadership role in World Council affairs. One of the parties to the 1918 merger, the United Synod of the South, rejoined the parent body after the healing of the rift developed during the Civil War.

This early concern for unity among American Lutherans, which developed during the World War I era, has continued unabated ever since. According to Frank S. Mead, "Since 1910 there has been an almost constant effort toward the unification of Lutheran Churches and agencies. . . . At one time there were 150 Lutheran bodies in the country." [49] Today the number is down to "around twenty"—probably eighteen separate groups.

Lutherans now form the third largest Protestant denomination in the nation. Several large-scale merger plans currently under negotiation, if successful, will further reduce the remaining Lutheran groups into two or three. One Lutheran official, the president of the National Lutheran Council, has advocated

[48] In contrast to other Lutheran groups, this judgment seems correct, despite the heresy trials of three Wisconsin pastors in 1955.

[49] *Handbook of Denominations in the United States* (Nashville: Abingdon Press, 1956), pp. 130-32. Also cf. F. E. Mayer, *The Religious Bodies in America* (St. Louis: Concordia Publishing House, 1954), pp. 178-89.

a radical plan "to scrap two of the merger plans under negotiation in favor of a single, all-inclusive church." This proposal would unite seven major bodies representing two thirds of the Lutherans in America. His "over-all merger proposal" was finally rejected, however, lest it "scuttle two merger efforts already well advanced in negotiation."

Clearly, Lutheran groups in America have changed in posture and practice from proliferation to consolidation. What role do social factors play in this switch?

Since many Lutheran groups derive their existence from *ethnic diversities,* including the numerous foreign language groups which arrived in successive immigrant waves, one of the chief reasons for their multiplicity may be traced to the impact of social factors. So writes one Lutheran leader: "Poor communications and consequent isolation of nations and churches from each other . . . differences in race and language, intense nationalism, diversity in economic interest, and national alignment are among the causes which have separated the Evangelical Lutheran Churches." [50]

Immigrant Lutheran groups landing in America included Norwegians, Danish, Finnish, Swedish, Slovak, Poles, Dutch, Icelandic, and various German groups. These newcomers transplanted their own ethnic, foreign-language churches, which in turn split into other segments on the American soil. As European cultural ties slowly erode and assimilation to American culture accelerates (a process earlier examined), much of the original social basis for Lutheran diversity disappears. In this process of acculturation, English becomes the predominant language; with the curtailment of immigration, the foreign language recedes into the background, only to linger with the first and second generations.

As assimilation proceeds, churches discard their ethnic label, or more significantly, replace it with an American symbol. Such was the case for the Norwegian Church of America, as well

[50] Quoted by H. Paul Douglass, *A Decade of Objective Progress in Church Unity, 1927-1936* (New York: Harper & Brothers, 1937), p. 22.

as the Danish Evangelical Lutheran Church, which also dropped its nationality reference adopting the name American Evangelical Lutheran Church in 1953. One of the pending merger proposals, scheduled for consummation on January 1, 1961, will bring together three groups, each springing from different ethnic sources: Evangelical Lutheran Church (Norwegian), American Lutheran Church (German), and United Evangelical Lutheran Church (Danish). Apart from other imperatives for unity, certainly the lessening of social differences and the mounting allegiance to a commonly shared culture must be acknowledged.

At the local level, the changing significance of an ethnic label may be gleaned from this remark voiced by an official of the Augustana Evangelical Lutheran Church: "We used to be thought of by our own members, as well as by people in the community, as 'the Swedish Church on 22nd Street!' But now, as our older members are dying off, the national label is disappearing." [51]

Erasing the ethnic label is one way to remove the stigma of immigrant, foreign status in the quest for cultural Americanization. It also attracts other groups who might otherwise be alienated as the denomination appeals more widely for membership. Since an ethnic Lutheran church cannot replenish its membership with immigrants, and in view of changing neighborhood populations, it must resort to evangelization and recruitment from the ranks of those not traditionally tied to the church of immigrant descent. A recent survey of Lutheran churches in the New York metropolitan area found that out of 167 churches reporting, eighty parishes are interracial; one congregation has twenty-eight nationalities represented in its membership, and another twenty-two. "Now that we have convinced ourselves," confesses a document of the Lutheran Church, "we

[51] Quoted in *Time Magazine*, April 7, 1958. Significantly, *Time's* feature article in this issue was called "The New Lutheran," and dealt with the signs of unity among American Lutherans. In some metropolitan areas, Lutherans are the most aggressive denomination in fostering multi-racial, inclusive church memberships.

are by our actions trying to convince non-Lutherans that to label the local Lutheran Church, the 'German,' the 'Swedish,' the 'Norwegian,' the 'Danish,' the 'Finnish,' is actually inaccurate. The Lutheran Church is now . . . an American Lutheran Church, not simply a transplantation of the Lutheran Church of other lands." [52]

To reiterate by way of summary: in view of the gradual shedding of ethnic identification, the breakdown of geographical and sectional isolation, the increased loyalty to American culture—precipitated partly by two world wars, when loyalty to certain foreign nations was viewed with suspicion—and the assimilation of succeeding generations, the social bases for the numerous Lutheran bodies have been radically altered. Such erosion of social differences and common allegiance to an emerging cultural unity constitute important social sources for church unity. Indeed, instead of the multiplicity of Lutheran groups, momentum has been swiftly gathering for organic union among Lutherans in America. Social conditions have contributed significantly by enabling this new movement toward unity.

A third merger of Lutheran synods, which we shall consider next, involves the Lutheran Synod of Buffalo, Evangelical Lutheran Synod of Iowa and Other States, and Evangelical. Lutheran Joint Synod of Ohio and Other States. Adopting the name American Lutheran Church, this consolidation of the synods of Iowa, Ohio, and Buffalo in 1930 was later joined by the Texas synod.[53]

Historically these four synods, though separated geographically, shared one common characteristic: they worked primarily with German Lutheran immigrants. Such common ethnic identification might have drawn these groups together earlier were

---

[52] Omar Bonderud and Charles Lutz, eds., *American Lutherans* (Columbus, Ohio: Wartburg Press, 1955) , p. 6.

[53] For a detailed historical study of this merger, cf. Fred W. Meuser, *The Formation of the American Lutheran Church* (Columbus, Ohio: Wartburg Press, 1958) .

it not for the fact that members of the separate synods arrived at different times with different waves of immigration. Merger was to await assimilation to American culture.

Although the American Lutheran Church is generally regarded as a bulwark of Germans, its founders were mainly born in America. Due to the vast influx of Germans after 1830, the synods actually became more German as the century advanced. With respect to the use of German as a foreign language, however, the process reversed itself. The *1926 Census of Religious Bodies* (prior to the merger) reports on this reversal in the Synod of Iowa and Other States:

In its early history the Synod used the German language . . . but of late years the use of English has increased steadily. A number of congregations of native-born Americans have been formed; a church paper in English has been prepared. During the last decade, the English language became dominant. Many congregations use it exclusively, and there are very few which do not employ it at all. The General Assembly has ruled that only bi-lingual ministers can join the Synod.[54]

Ties to European homelands have become increasingly tenuous. Today the American Lutheran Church has become more Americanized, while remaining predominantly rural. Its German heritage is still evident in some ways. A biweekly German paper published by the church has a circulation of 4,500, but this is tiny compared to the denomination's English weekly, *The Lutheran Standard,* which goes into more than 100,000 homes. Both world wars hastened the switch from a German-speaking to an essentially English-speaking church. Thus the American Lutheran Church has pursued the interesting course of progressively becoming more German, and then gradually becoming less so, as its orientation broadens. Like other ethnic Lutheran denominations, the acculturation process has grad-

[54] *Census of Religious Bodies, 1926* (Washington, D. C.: United States Government Printing Office, 1929), p. 95.

ually eroded the distinctive cultural heritage of the American Lutheran Church.[55]

Active in unity movements among Lutherans, the American Lutheran Church conceives of its role as a mediating force, maintaining friendly contacts with both the United Lutheran Church to the left and the Synodical Conference to the right. It was instrumental in organizing the "American Lutheran Conference" in 1930, a confederation which also included these ethnic expressions of Lutheranism—Swedish Augustana, Lutheran Free Church (Norwegian), United Danish Church, and the Norwegian Church of America.

Lutheran church historian Fred W. Meuser cites the formation of the American Lutheran Conference as "evidence of the Americanization of the Swedish, Danish, Norwegian, and German synods." [56] In addition, the American Lutheran Church enjoys close relationships with the Missouri Synod, with which it is currently working toward doctrinal agreement. As previously noted, by 1961 the American Lutheran Church will become a part of a still larger Lutheran merger. Lutheran groups are no longer enclaves in American life. Assimilation to a common-core American culture has made easier the merging of these once diverse and divided Lutheran bodies.

B. UNITED CHURCH OF CHRIST. For our case study of a trans-denominational-merger, we turn next to the United Church of Christ, which joined the Congregational-Christian Churches with the Evangelical and Reformed Church. Fashioned by the 1957 Uniting Synod, this new body, numbering over 2,000,000 (1,401,565 Congregational-Christians and 807,280 Evangelical and Reformed), became the seventh largest Protestant group in the United States.

Complicated by legal entanglements, factions, and maneuvers on both sides, arguments advanced for the merger differ in in-

---

[55] For a further discussion of this point, see the chapter entitled "The Norwegians: Sect and Ethnic Groups," in W. Lloyd Warner, *Democracy in Jonesville, op. cit.,* pp. 168-92.

[56] *Op. cit.,* p. 249.

terpretation according to one's prior position. Although an objective historical account is beyond the immediate scope of this study, our analysis of social factors cannot bypass controversial issues surrounding the merger.

In general, the pro-merger forces contend that the two parties to the union complement each other in historical background, geographical distribution, and polity. On the other hand, the antimerger group argues that such diversities are incompatible and tend to dilute historic congregationalism. Vociferous "continuing bodies" have organized to contest and reject the merger.

Historically, the two groups represent partners to several previous unions. Of British stock, the Congregationalists trace their beginning to the arrival of the English Pilgrims on the Mayflower in 1620. The Christian Churches, joining the Congregationalists in 1931, began in the early nineteenth century among American Baptists, Methodists, and Presbyterians who were of British stock as well.

For the Evangelical and Reformed, the pioneers of the Reformed Church came to this country from the Rhinelands and the German Swiss countries in the eighteenth century; small groups also emanated from France and Holland. The Evangelical Synod is derived from the Evangelical United Church of Prussia, which in turn represents a union of the Lutheran and Reformed traditions by mandate of King Frederick William III. Hence the merger of Congregational-Christians and the Evangelical and Reformed drew together the sons and daughters of the British and of the Continental Reformation.

In addition to differing historical streams, the geographical distribution of the two merged bodies is also complementary. Congregationalists have their center of strength in New England, while the Christians arose largely from the great revivals in Tennessee and Kentucky, with some representation in North Carolina as well. Evangelical and Reformed are strong in the Middle West, with the Evangelicals substantial in the Mississippi Valley and Missouri area and the Reformed counting their strength in the Pennsylvania and Ohio areas.

Little difference exists between the two groups in theology and ritual, despite creedal charges alleged by some Congregationalists. But in the realm of polity (i.e., church government and decision-making processes), historical differences distinguish the two parties to the merger. This contrasting polity furnished one of the major bones of contention for dyed-in-the-wool Congregationalists.

Historically, Congregational-Christians stress the autonomy of the local church, whereas the Evangelical and Reformed have a more articulate form of regional synods. In early conceptions of Congregationalism, the status of the local church was central. As previously discussed, however, rapid social changes in organizational life demand the functional adaptation of polities, until they become more nearly identical in their performance of responsibilities and execution of policies.

To keep abreast of the developing frontier, the rise of urbanization, the denomination's geographical dispersion, and the social and technological revolution some form of more centralized and unified system was found necessary. In a nation increasingly characterized by organizational development and the centralization of organizations in nearly all institutional walks of life, a denomination declines and weakens without benefit of co-ordinated and articulated direction and plans of action.

Around the middle of the nineteenth century Congregational churches felt the need for firmer organizational development and initiated movements toward national consolidation. Once formed, the "logic of institutional development" entails the assumption of more and more important and necessary functions on the part of the centralized agency.[57] Meanwhile, for the tradition-minded minority, an inherent dilemma ensues. The autonomy of the local congregation, it fears, suffers at the expense of national organization. The majority, however, carried

[57] Cf. Robert Michels, *Political Parties* (Chicago: The Free Press of Glencoe, Ill., 1951).

113

by the ecumenical tide, desires that Congregational-Christians should keep abreast of developing institutional forms which best perform essential tasks dictated by the new cultural situation. Epitomizing this sentiment, Douglas Horton, one of the architects of the merger, contends that the developed form of Congregationalism is alone adequate for present-day needs:

The older type may have been effectual in the days of an agrarian economy, when the village was the pivotal point of the nation's life. . . . Now, however, in order to out-guess and out-maneuver anti-Christian forces which are organized at higher levels than that of the village or local district, it is necessary to have a flexible church unit with sufficient authority over itself to be able to act unrestrictedly at those levels.[58]

In similar vein, Henry P. Van Dusen avers:

In an earlier day when many Christian's lives were circumscribed by the affairs of their local community, the extreme "congregational" ideal of the Church as a local association of individual Christians might have sufficed. . . . Today two factors have rendered it obsolete: the reclamation of a deeper awareness of the organic interrelatedness of humanity—the concept of "community"—and the inescapable emergence of interrelatedness in the modern world. It may be doubted whether any major Christian group—save the more perverse American Southern Baptists—still hold the *congregation* to be an adequate ideal for the organized Christian Church.[59]

Thus in a changing society, new institutional patterns are found necessary for the denomination to keep up with the organizational revolution and the functional interdependence earlier reviewed. In large measure, these social sources have modified historic congregationalism, readying it for organic union.

Recalling our earlier discussion of the convergence of organi-

[58] Quoted by Rouse and Neill, *op. cit.*, p. 482.
[59] *World Christianity* (Nashville: Abingdon Press, 1947) , p. 225.

zational structures, we should not be surprised to learn that fewer differences characterize the two merging parties than are commonly assumed. While one is presbyterian and the other congregational, in actual practice many similar features are evident in the evolving organizational structure of both denominations on the American scene. Confirmation of this development grew out of the experience of the two negotiating groups. They found that in many areas of church life, the Evangelical and Reformed were more responsive to the will of local congregations and more dependent upon a system of local representation on committees; contrariwise, while Congregationalists rely more on local autonomy theoretically, it was discovered that actually the national denominational staff was free from explicit guidance or required representation from local churches in numerous areas.

Realization of the need for increased organizational leadership to carry out large-scale responsibilities and the functional similarities of seemingly diverse polities have mitigated earlier fears expressed by some of the reluctant antagonists.

Adoption of a constitution for the merged group is scheduled for a special synod meeting in the summer of 1960. An affirmation of faith, which many feel embodies a fresh statement of ecumenical theology, was approved at the second synod meeting in the summer of 1959. Although another round of litigation will challenge the merger, there is every expectation that the United Church of Christ will emerge a victorious reality.

Since the antimerger forces constitute such a vital part in making the road to union a sometimes rocky journey, we must devote some attention to the organized opposition.

In the fall of 1948 the minority antimerger group organized the "National Anti-Merger Committee," which was subsequently succeeded by the "Committee for the Continuation of Congregational-Christian Churches of the United States." Another splinter group against the merger, the "Conservative Congregational Conference" began as a reaction against the denomination's "liberal leadership." Still another antimerger organization

115

is the "League to Uphold Congregational Principles." Finally, in November, 1955, the "National Association of Congregational-Christian Churches in the United States" was founded in Detroit by antimerger representatives of 106 local churches. In covering this Detroit meeting a *Christian Century* editor wrote a stinging caricature, which did little to endear him to the hearts of antimergerites:

> They came breathing fire at the proposal to write a constitution for Congregationalism, and promptly wrote one for themselves. . . . This group shoved around and manipulated the most incredible superficialities. If a new church is born of such parentage, it will be the lightest-weight sect of Christendom. Oh, how these Christians need the church they so lightly dismiss! [60]

The National Association of Congregational-Christian Churches may well develop into a splinter group, carrying on the name of the original body. In such an event, we might hazard the prediction that, in the course of time, when the storm abates and old memories fade away, the splinter group will seek reunion with its parent body—particularly if all the fears of "galloping authoritarianism" are proved groundless. Meanwhile emotions are riding high. Antimerger parties remain separate for the sake of perpetuating several values:

Chief among these values are the "traditions and principles of historic Congregationalism." In the "Articles of Association" of the National Association, the new group's purpose is stated: "To aid . . . the continuance and growth of those things which by tradition and practice have been the historic and accepted characteristics of Congregational-Christian Churches." Particular emphasis is placed, as someone puts it, "in the Holy Local Church."

Another set of values centers around the terms "freedom" and "fellowship," concepts which convey different meaning among various leaders of the antimerger forces. For some it

[60] Editorial, "Movement or Machination," *Christian Century* (November 23, 1955).

means an appeal to the diversity of witness as the "essence of Protestantism." For others it connotes autonomy, a citadel of democracy, struggling for its survival against the encroachment of "centralization," "bureaucracy," and "authoritarianism." Many view it as the freedom of the local congregation—a value dramatically set forth in a widely disseminated pamphlet picturing a huge hand about to seize a small church in its rapacious grip. Under the scene is this caption, "They're Planning to Take Your Church." Sponsored by two antimerger groups, this handbook warns in bold-faced type: "Your Church Will Lose Its Present Freedom"; "The New Denomination Will Be an *Authoritarian Church*"; "Your Church Will Lose Its Identity as a *Free Independent* Church"; "Your Church Will Lose Its Real *Autonomy*"; "We Will Lose Our Bodies of *Free Fellowship.*"

To generalize and say that the antimerger forces are also opposed to social action as conducted by the denomination's Council for Social Action may be erroneous. Nevertheless, during the controversy over the status and character of the Council for Social Action, some of the same individuals opposed to union were also contending against the Council. Moreover, Dr. James Fifield, a leader of "Spiritual Mobilization," a religious fellowship with a right-wing economic slant, is a conspicuous leader in antimerger organizations. One antimerger group is responsible for circulating reprints of J. B. Matthews' *American Mercury* article, which indiscriminately labeled many prominent Protestant clergymen as fellow travelers.

Many in antimerger circles would not agree that essential theological agreement obtains between Congregationalists and Evangelical and Reformed. A frequently proclaimed slogan warned: "Mergers Meant Creeds!" Behind the union movement, some charged, lurked a sinister "neo-orthodox theology," which would undercut liberalism and endanger the freedom of the church. Thus asserted Marion J. Bradshaw, formerly of Bangor Theological Seminary, in a book entitled *Baleful Legacy*.[61] In

[61] (Oklahoma City: Modern Publishers, Inc.. 1955), pp. 4, 9, 87, *passim.*

polemical overtones, Bradshaw appealed to Congregational-Christians to steer clear of neo-orthodoxy, which he linked with prounionists, and expressed grave fears, lest the proposed United Church endanger the autonomy of individual Congregational Churches.

Proponents of the merger claim that it represents a real break-through in the history of American Protestant church unions. Being a transconfessional union, it successfully bridges diverse backgrounds—historically, ethnically, geographically, and polity-wise. These differences have been largely transcended on the American scene. Allegiance to a common American culture and a common-core Protestantism has replaced the earlier dissimilarities.

To be sure, dissident elements have resisted and sought to block the merger. Their dissidence too is, in part, based on social sources. Significantly though, the trend in the unitive direction is steadier and stronger. Doubtless a minority view is reflected in a letter to *Advance,* the denomination's magazine, in which the writer expresses his antipathy for joining with Germans and Continentals: "We of the English lineage could not forever and amicably fit in with those of Continental lineage.[62] For the overwhelming majority, ethnic diversities have either been overcome or are pointed to with pride as something quite remote and, indeed, rather quaint. In fact the information secretary for the merger once said in a public address, "Now that we are *American enough,* we can all unite." [63] Signs are already apparent that the day is not far distant when other denominations—possibly Disciples of Christ and the American Baptists —will join forces with the United Church of Christ.

IV. SUMMARY

In our account of organic church unions, we have observed that a number of social factors are at work contributing to their

[62] F. P. Strong, "Letter to the Editor," *Advance* (November, 1946).
[63] Lecture at Union Theological Seminary, New York City, Spring, 1954.

consummation. Various social strands run through these mergers. They will be briefly highlighted in successive paragraphs.

With increased cultural Americanization, the older barriers once separating religious groups have been minimized; hence groups of different ethnic backgrounds—or similar groups arriving in America at different periods—are no longer dependent upon an ethnic base for their survival. Former ethnic ties and alien features have dissolved, as allegiance centers on American culture. This process of the molding of diversities into a unitive pattern finds expression in religious institutional life as Protestants seek an adequate organizational means for implementing the new-found cultural unity.

Just as the ethnic label is discarded, so too sectional labels fall aside. Denominations may seek other groups to complement their work in their desire to span the continent. This suggests the diminution of sectional and geographical barriers. Increased consciousness of national unity, aided by common exposure to norms and values stemming from the mass media, have mitigated the spirit of sectionalism. For example, the self-image of Congregationalists—that of a "white-upper-middle-class-Yankee New Englander"—is gradually being shattered and revealed as a distorted image. Congregationalism has willy-nilly moved far beyond New England and finds itself ministering to a multiplicity of ethnic groups.

Among the unavowed social sources of organic mergers is the status factor. Certainly the publicity materials relating to mergers hardly ever fail to announce the numerical size and rank of the proposed union, if consummated—"the third largest" or the "sixth largest" group in American Protestantism. In addition to the status derived from size, there is the status which stems from upward mobility. Smaller bodies may ascend in status by affiliation with prestige and status-laden groups. Status goals, of course, operate in subtle and covert ways as a contributing social source of church union.

With increased size, enabled by mergers, also goes greater institutional power. Frequently evangelistic "quotas" set by

119

denominations are less concerned with the Christian care and nurture of converts, than with the institutional expansion and strengthening of the particular group. Mergers enhance the potential for wielding institutional power both in relation to other churches and to the secular currents in society at large.

Not least among the unavowed social sources of organic union comes economic efficiency. Of course, the other side of this coin is the minimization of competition—the kind of costly competition which similarly induces business interests to merge and consolidate. This latent support for church unity that stems from the nature of competition as a social process is not widely admitted or acknowledged by church leaders. When recognized, the role of competition is stated gingerly and apologetically. Hence Douglas Horton, in reference to the merger of the United Church of Christ, declared:

The most obvious advantage of the union is the least important and has been the least frequently mentioned: the union will constitute an out-and-out benefit to the business life of the two communions. All the features of denominational life which depend upon what is called commercially the size of the market or the breadth of the financial base will be profitted. It costs relatively little more, for instance, to publish and circulate a magazine for 500,000 subscribers than for a tenth of that number. Ministers' pension schemes will be actuarially more sound when they serve larger numbers. In the United Church of Christ there will be over 2,100,000 members and about 8,500 ministers. These will provide market opportunities and financial advantages which no businessman would deny.[64]

Thus the economic advantages of merger, both in savings and in more adequate deployment of resources, play a latent role in their consummation.

Of the two types of organic unions, it appears that the intra-denominational type is more common, and perhaps more char-

[64] Copyright 1957 Christian Century Foundation. Reprinted by permission from *The Christian Century*.

acteristic of the earlier part of the twentieth century. Most of these unions and reunions have effectively bridged what were once social chasms. These social differences which underlay separation have been largely reduced or modified in the common adaptation of the various religious groups to American culture. Hence religious divisions, which were primarily social in their particular source, have now ceased to be meaningful, as these social sources—nationality, ethnic, language, sectional, geographical, rural-urban, and class differences—are transcended. The reduction of these social diversities provides the social sources of church unity.

By way of implication, the following exploratory and tentative observations may be added:

1. Other things being equal, groups which complement one another geographically find it easier to merge their forces. This represents a changed attitude, from regarding churches located in different areas of the nation as lacking in affinity, to the belief that such differential location strengthens the denomination as a national body and gives it more adequate national status.

2. Common origins in ethnic, historical, and doctrinal identity facilitated the earlier attempts at organic union. These mergers are based on similarities within denominational families—similarities which may have been obscured by added layers of social characteristics, only to be realized through later common cultural identification. At the earlier stage, organic mergers are not yet capable of joining groups of diverse traditions and backgrounds.

3. Some of the more recent organic unions—and prospective ones—bridge past social differences. They are based on growing similarities between denominations. The fact that these mergers are able to bridge past cultural differences suggests their external orientation—that is, their affinity to an emerging common American culture.

In the next chapter we come to grips with another sign and instrumentality of church unity, namely, councils of churches, as embodied in the national and local conciliar movement. We will examine the extent to which these councils have developed and become a firmly rooted part of religious life in America; our major focus of attention will also be on the role of social factors in the course of the development of the conciliar movement.

5. The Conciliar Movement

The chief locus of co-operative Protestantism in America is found in local councils of churches. These councils have become an established pattern of interchurch relationships in communities throughout the nation. For many American Protestants, their only personal acquaintance and contact with what they regard as the ecumenical movement comes through local councils of churches.

Sometimes called the "American brand of ecumenicity," or an "indigenous form of American ecumenicity," local councils received significant recognition as legitimate expressions of unity at the Oberlin Conference on Faith and Order.

I. NATIONAL COUNCIL OF CHURCHES

At the national level stands the National Council of Churches, successor organization to the Federal Council of Churches, whose historic beginnings have already been traced. Its chief purposes are: "To manifest oneness in Jesus Christ as Divine Lord and Savior, by the creation of an inclusive cooperating agency of the Christian churches in the United States . . . to continue and extend the . . . general agencies of the churches, and to combine all their interests and functions."

A result of the merger of thirteen interdenominational agencies, today the National Council comprises thirty-four church bodies with a combined membership of nearly 40,000,000. Thirty-five additional religious groups hold "associate" or

123

"affiliate" relationship status in one or more of the Council's various units. They include such diverse groups as the Advent Christian Church; Church of God, Anderson, Indiana; General Conference of the Mennonite Church; some boards and agencies of the Southern Baptist Convention; and Schwenkfelder.

Compared with the old Federal Council's original budget of 9,000 dollars in 1909, the National Council's 1959 anticipated budget stands at 21,459,470 dollars including the sum of 9,095,000 dollars earmarked for Church World Service's program of relief shipments.

1. Contributions of the National Council. Since its inception in 1950, the Council has rendered valuable services in numerous areas of the life and work of its related groups. Its contributions have been well summarized in a *Christian Century* editorial, which lists these accomplishments:

The National Council has brought nearly all the forms of Protestant and Orthodox inter-church cooperation into relation with each other in one organization.

The organization has advanced a good way into putting its own house in order and in winning for itself as the instrument of the churches freedom to consider and to speak publicly on national issues of current importance.

The Council has greatly advanced the study of the Bible by publishing the Revised Standard Version and by promoting its circulation and use.

The churches have aided each other in good works through the Council, whose Department of Church World Service has brought into this country 62,644 refugees and has sent out 55 million pounds of food, clothing, and medicine. . . .

The Council has organized chaplaincies on seagoing vessels and in the national parks.

The Council has set up 393 religious radio and TV programs, some continuing through the year, has opened religious radio stations . . . has completed the first city-wide study of the effect on TV on children and family life.

Its publishing program has issued more than a million books, has coordinated Sunday school materials for 35 million children, has developed and published a Sunday school curriculum for Spanish-speaking Americans.

Its work includes a million children in weekday schools of religion and three million in daily vacation Bible schools.

Its program serves 300,000 agricultural migrants and an equal number of people in atomic defense communities.

It has united 471 church colleges in a study of religion on the campuses. It serves 250 colleges with interdenominational religious programs.

It supervises and helps 50 overseas union churches for Americans living abroad.[1]

The National Council's impact on religious life in America cannot be adequately understood by merely listing its achievements. At best the above compilation is partial and omits such available services as racial and cultural relations, international justice, urban and rural work, and research and survey—all of which constitute major departments in the work of the Council.
2. Social factors. To a large degree, the social factors in the National Council's development are an extension and intensification of the same factors which prompted the rise of the Federal Council just after the turn of the century. In addition the increased interdependence of American society and the trend toward greater centralization of organizations must be recognized. Earlier, we noted the development of large-scale organizations as a response to the increased need for co-ordination and specialization in a technological society. Consider how the National Council has assumed functions which only a centralized, co-ordinated agency can perform effectively. The Council's specialized departments and services supplement the work of denominations and local churches and foster mutual dependence among these various bodies. Like other organizations and agencies of nation-wide scope, the Council can sponsor special observances and issue proclamations, such as "Race Relations Sunday" and "World Wide Communion Sunday." Just as certain

[1] Copyright 1954 Christian Century Foundation. Reprinted by permission from *The Christian Century*.

holidays and national observances sponsored by the national government bear the latent function of supporting the government, similarly, national observances in the religious realm, under the aegis of the National Council, function latently to support the Council itself.

Numerous social and cultural pressures demand the co-ordinated efforts of Protestantism through some such channel as the National Council. If the Protestant forces wish to "speak to the nation" on important social, political, and economic issues, they cannot do so effectively through the offices of fragmented churches. Some form of corporate expression and action is mandatory. As previously noted, this was one of the prime motivations of the Federal Council of Churches. In such areas of controversy as race relations, labor-management problems, nuclear weapons, economic abundance, "McCarthyism," and unemployment, the Council has centered attention. To the credit of a large organization like the National Council, it has taken significant stands on social questions, where other organizations of similar scope, in order to preserve institutional stability, may be reluctant to do so.

A structure like the National Council is necessary if Protestant groups are to carry out the many inevitable relationships with other institutions of society, national agencies, and the national government. In the program of religious services in national parks, or in work with refugees and displaced persons, imagine the chaotic consequences of an unco-ordinated program performed by a multiplicity of competing church bodies. Similarly, the government uses religious channels for relief work.

The military chaplaincy program begun by the Federal Council continues to be an important field of joint operation. In co-operation with the General Commission on Chaplains and Armed Forces Personnel, the federal government supports and administers a religious ministry to the personnel of the armed forces. During World War II the peak number of chaplains was in the neighborhood of 12,000.

The chaplaincy program has become a permanent one, governed by regulations, and the need for chaplains persists. What the significance of a government supported and supervised program of religious activities may be for local churches is a wide-open question; for increasingly the military chaplaincy has become a "full-orbed parish ministry" to men and their families. In a recent year 36,000 persons were baptized by military chaplains. What this means for those who did not elect baptism into a particular communion is uncertain. The effect of training and experience on the chaplain's own future civilian church leadership calls for study. There are hints that sometimes men with such experience feel emancipated from denominational ties and find it difficult to return to a local denominational church setting. They may therefore choose teaching, institutional chaplaincy, or the college chaplaincy. Reported also are cases of chaplains who transfer to other denominations. The precise number, and whether this is directly related to chaplaincy experience, or to other causes, has not been determined.

Moreover, we know little about the effect of the "general Protestant worship service," the widespread integration and mixing of people from different denominational backgrounds, interdenominational Bible study groups, a unified Sunday-school curriculum, and interdenominational lay leadership programs. Yet, by way of speculation, it is highly probable that the chaplaincy program in its impact on both clergymen and laymen tends to foster a non-denominational, common-core Protestantism, which eventually reinforces ecumenicity in the local community.

To cite one more area where joint operation is necessary, consider the radio and television field, which is under the guidance of the Broadcasting and Film Commission of the National Council. The Commission presents programs on 585 radio and 550 TV stations weekly. In addition to films and filmstrips, it produces five radio and nine TV programs weekly. The Commission maintains an important liaison with the broadcasting and film industries.

Network policy designates responsibility to the legitimately constituted and recognized national church body for broadcast time on a sustaining basis. In consequence not only do various denominations work co-operatively in a common project, but also, the message, as projected to vast audiences numbering in the millions, is free of sectarian and denominational bias. Audiences are thus confronted with a common religious pattern, which contributes to the underlying soil from which, in part, grows the church unity movement in America.

Apart from the functional needs fulfilled by a national agency of Protestant denominations, some argue that a strong National Council is the Protestant response to the concentrated power vested in a unified hierarchical force, as represented by Roman Catholicism. John T. McNeill wrote "The rising strength of Roman Catholicism with its example of solid unity . . . may be forcing us unwillingly to clasp each other's hands." [2] In general, ecumenical literature does not abound with references to united Protestantism as a counterforce to Roman Catholic power. Such dearth may reflect the fact that the issue is often joined with fears that Catholicism constitutes a threat to American democracy, and militant anti-Catholicism is viewed in more discriminating Protestant circles as frequently irresponsible.[3]

The absence of references pointing to Protestant unity as a way of counteracting the cohesiveness of Roman Catholic organization makes this phenomenon more difficult to identify as a contributing source of ecumenicity. Occasionally, a dramatic instance—such as protest against sending an ambassador to the Vatican—highlights the effectiveness of unified Protestant action. Perhaps in the minds of some Protestants, enthusiasm

---

[2] "Protestantism," *Religion and Our Divided Denominations*, ed. W. L. Sperry (Cambridge, Mass.: Harvard University Press, 1945), p. 68. For a more vigorous statement of this viewpoint cf. Paul Blanshard, *American Freedom and Catholic Power* (Boston: Beacon Press, 1949).

[3] In contrast to serving as a counterforce, the National Council is sometimes attacked for being overly friendly toward Roman Catholicism. Cf. James DeForest Murch, *Cooperation Without Compromise* (Grand Rapids: Wm. B. Eerdmans Publishing Company, 1956), pp. 15, 137, 184, 207; and Carl McIntire, *Twentieth Century Reformation* (Collingwood: Christian Beacon Press, 1946). See especially Chapter VIII, entitled, "The Big Sister."

for the ecumenical movement is enhanced by the assurance that it represents an actual or potential bulwark against Roman Catholic strength. The evidence that this feeling prevails, however, or that it plays a decisive role in the development of church unity is scanty. Doubtless it remains a latent source. As Gustave Weigel, Jesuit scholar of Woodstock College, contends, "The overall compactness of the Catholic group is impressive, too impressive for the comfort of non-Catholics who groundlessly live with the fear of future Catholic dominance of the land." [4]

At the local community level, the appeal to Protestant unity to counter Roman Catholic influence is more discernible. In his massive study of Protestant and Catholic relationships in Holyoke, Massachusetts, Kenneth Underwood describes how a local council conducted a meeting which made a vigorous appeal for a united stand against Roman Catholic institutional strength:

> At the most carefully prepared and widely attended meeting ever held by the Protestant Council of Churches in Paper City, the main speaker described the "rising tide of Catholic Power in America," and concluded that "individual denominations can alone do nothing against it. A *united stand* against Catholics' claim that theirs is the only true church must be made." . . . "There is no hope in the world except in fellowship." [5]

Protestants will rally around their own organized centers of power in contesting Roman Catholic claims, especially in dealing with such recurrent issues as bingo, birth control practices and policies (e.g., in city-operated hospitals) , and aid to parochial schools. Particularly in communities where Roman Catholicism is the dominant religious group, one might expect to find Protestants organized in ministerial associations or local councils of churches, ready to preserve and defend their interests against competing claims and eager to augment their own institutional strengths through united endeavors.

The National Council's program and policies increasingly

[4] "American Roman Catholicism and Ecumenism," *Lutheran World*, V (June, 1958) , 30.
[5] *Protestant and Catholic* (Boston: Beacon Press, 1957) , p. 112.

take on added significance for the life of local churches and denominations. Already noted are its direct contributions and service functions. Not so obvious to the average church member, however, is the National Council's representation of local churches in the great power centers of society where far-reaching decisions are forged. As division of labor and the "nucleation process" earlier reviewed continue in American society, local churches and laymen will come to depend more and more on the work of the National Council of Churches.

II. LOCAL COUNCILS OF CHURCHES

The relationship between the National Council and autonomous local councils has progressively become closer, according to the National Council's 1954 biennial report:

> Real progress has been made in achieving a consistent and sound pattern of relationships between the National Council and state and local councils. Those few state and local councils that have not traditionally been based upon the principles of the National Council . . . have been gradually adjusting their structures and operations in the direction of conformity to the basic principles of the National Council.[6]

One of the National Council's major units, the Office for Councils of Churches, works intimately with local councils, providing consultation and assistance in program planning and evaluation and in financial and personnel matters. This office serves as a clearinghouse for the scattered local councils across the nation. It co-operates closely with the Association of Council Secretaries, a professional organization of council personnel, which meets annually for a week to consider concerns of the conciliar movement.[7]

[6] *Biennial Report* (New York: National Council of Churches, 1954), p. 33.
[7] "Conciliar movement" is an expression which has come into general usage to refer to councils of churches. In this study, it is not to be confused with the more traditional historical usages, as referring to the seven great Ecumenical Councils in the early history of the Church, or to the movement associated with

Affinity between the National and the local councils can also be traced historically through the Federal Council. A number of local councils antedate the Federal Council, although it is commonly assumed that the Federal Council stimulated the development of local councils through the Commission on State and Local Federations. Authorized at the Council's Second Quadrennial in 1912, this commission sought to fulfill one of the Federal Council's stated objectives, namely, "to assist in the organization of local branches of the Federal Council to promote its aims in their communities." Yet some evidence shows that local councils already in existence helped to provide the impetus for the founding of the Federal Council.

As the constituting convention of the Federal Council in 1908, Ame Vennema, a former president of the General Synod of the Reformed Church in America, said to the delegates:

These interdenominational organizations [local councils] are pioneers in the field; they have broken ground; they have blazed the way, and have helped to make possible the work which this [Federal] Council contemplates doing.

These interdenominational organizations are the children of the Church . . . and they are introducing the churches themselves and bringing them into closer relations with each other. I believe, sirs, that this Council could not have been convened, except for the fact that through these interdenominational organizations, the churches have been working together side by side for so long a time. . . . In recognition of that fact the first Resolution is offered:

That it is the sense of this Council that the interdenominational organizations of the United States by co-operative work along special lines of Christian effort, have done much to prepare the way for that broader co-operative work contemplated by this body.[8]

John of Paris and Marsiglio of Padua, in the fourteenth century, concerning the authority of representative church councils over against that of the monarchical papacy.

[8] Quoted by Raymond A. Gray, "The Ecumenical Necessity" (Unpublished Master of Sacred Theology dissertation, Union Theological Seminary, 1958), p. 22. Gray's thesis is one of the few recent studies of the work of local councils of churches.

While the Federal Council gradually grew in organizational stability the early local councils lacked durability. Twenty-one known federations (as the movement was called during the first two decades of this century) were organized prior to 1900.[9] But when H. Paul Douglas sought to trace the historical development of these councils, he discovered that only those of New York City and Massachusetts had a continuous, uninterrupted life under a paid staff from the time of their origin.[10] All the other cities failed to recognize the continuity of their councils with those founded in the earlier period.

It would be intriguing to speculate on the reasons for this discontinuity between the earlier and later councils. Perhaps the earlier ones lacked a sufficiently broad base of community interest and lay support. A community acceptance and "social readiness" seem necessary before innovations like the pioneer councils can become institutionalized. The demise of a group of federations initiated by the Federal Council's staff suggests also the importance of an indigenous felt need within a community. Moreover, the early councils, in view of vocational uncertainty, were unable to attract highly competent professional leadership. Coupled with personnel turnover, this lack of exceptionally able local staff gave the movement a degree of instability.

The significant history of local councils, like most of the other organized expressions of church unity in America, can be dated from the beginning of the twentieth century. In fact, only within the last two decades have local councils become a firm institutional reality. Table 7 indicates the local conciliar movement's rapid growth in recent decades.

---

[9] Douglass, *Protestant Cooperation in American Cities*, p. 47. Important forerunners of the conciliar movement were the Evangelical Alliance and the Sunday School movement, from which many councils evolved. Local councils also grew out of ministerial associations, though the precise number is an unknown fact. In a few cases, state councils developed from state home missions councils. For a discussion of this relationship cf. Handy, *op. cit.*, pp. 48-63.

[10] *Ibid.*, p. 48.

TABLE 7
GROWTH OF LOCAL COUNCILS OF CHURCHES,
1917-1956 [11]

Year	City Councils With Paid Staff	City Councils Volunteer Staff
1917	c. 31	no data
1919	c. 40	no data
1921	c. 60	no data
1930	c. 50	no data
1941	98	87
1943	116	230
1945	147	354
1947	257	420
1956	281	657

Local councils now number approximately 938, located in communities across the land. Beginning in 1943, and particularly since 1945, their growth has been phenomenal. In the decade between 1945 and 1955, the local conciliar movement increased 300 per cent. In addition to these local councils, forty-four states have state councils, all but three of which have paid, professional leadership.[12] Compare this with the 1927 situation, when only four states had fully organized state councils. When one adds to the previously cited figures 2,157 councils of church women, 119 councils of church men, and 2,255 local ministerial associations, he cannot help but conclude that the conciliar movement is indeed of sizeable proportions.

Not only has there been extensive growth in the number of councils, but also long established councils have strengthened

[11] The early figures are approximations. Official records began to be taken in 1941. Sources of Data: *Workbook* for the Fourth Triennial Assembly of the National Council of Churches, 1957; J. Edward Lantz, "Church Councils in the South," *The Pastor* (August, 1956); and J. Quinter Miller, *Christian Unity: Its Relevance to the Community* (Shenandoah Publishing House, 1957), p. 16.
[12] State councils are not discussed here, though they form an important intermediary link between the National and the local councils.

their positions and grown intensively. For example—since budget figures provide one clue to growth—the Church Federation of Chicago has increased its budget from 38,000 dollars in 1942 to over 300,000 dollars in 1956. In the next five years, the Chicago Federation expects to increase its budget to 500,000 dollars. Such a development within a twenty-year period certainly heralds intensive growth. According to the Federation's executive director, plans for doubling the program in the next five years are largely in response to the vast social changes which already envelop the exploding Chicago metropolis. To anticipate our discussion, in large measure, these rapid social changes provide the occasion as well as the challenge and opportunity for broadening the sphere of action of the Chicago Church Federation, and, indeed, of the conciliar movement as a whole.

Increasingly the organizational work of councils draws upon the time and talents of lay leaders from local churches. In one way or another, the work of local councils probably touches the lives of some 40,000,000 Protestants; it involves some 500,000 lay people in positions of leadership, and consumes a total income of over 10,500,000 dollars per year. Hence the conciliar movement has grown from a weak and struggling institution to one of gigantic proportions. The end is not in view, for new communities are announcing new councils. Some of the major seminaries have launched training programs in council leadership as a special vocational field.

How does one account for the fact that the local conciliar movement has "won its way" in the religious institutional life of American Protestantism?

III. ROLE OF SOCIAL FACTORS

Although the National Council's leadership in stimulating the growth of new local councils should not be minimized, quite possibly both the National Council and local councils have developed and intensified their work as a response to social and cultural factors. These factors have already been examined with respect to the Federal and National Councils, and the points previously indicated are more or less applicable in considering local councils as well.

A. COMMUNITY-WIDE CO-ORDINATION. Whereas the National Council bears responsibility for a nation-wide orientation, local councils have a community-wide reference. Just as the National Council co-operates with the federal government and national agencies, so also local councils work with municipal governments and local agencies. For example, it would be inconceivable for a local board of education to deal with twenty-five separate denominations in planning for a released-time weekday religious education program.

Like its national counterpart, the local conciliar movement is in large measure born of the increased interdependence of American society, with the consequent necessity for functional co-ordination of the numerous existing organizations in the community. Local councils have been viewed as community clearinghouses of the churches for consultation and joint projects. Indeed, as is sometimes said, local councils are to the religious life of a community what the chamber of commerce is to its business life.

Seen in this perspective, local councils are organizational devices, ordering, integrating, and co-ordinating the diversity of Protestant church life in the community. They constitute a rational structure which emerges from a social context of multiple religious groups functioning in the American community. Their wider acceptance today springs partly from the fact that they fulfill a necessary and valuable function; they "plug a gap" in interchurch relationships. Through a trial and error process, the new machinery has been tested and found workable as a means for confronting the situation of institutional complexity and religious heterogeneity.

The necessity for *co-ordination* at the community level can be seen from an examination of the organizational development of innumerable local councils. A typical council begins by combining pre-existing agencies for church co-operation, unless it starts *de novo*. Usually there is an amalgamation of such commissions and agencies as a Sunday-school association, a social action commission, an interdenominational evangelistic committee, and a comity commission. These various agencies may have all appealed to a similar source for aid and support. Hence it becomes mutually advantageous to merge their interests and to gather their support from denominational channels. The council becomes a more inclusive body. Earlier independent agencies become departments or divisions in the organizational structure of the new council. As additional functions are assumed, other departments and commissions are attached to the structure—research, social welfare, radio-TV broadcasting, publications.

This gathering up of previous interdenominational agencies, and the inclusion of new departments into a more inclusive movement accounts for some degree of "built-in inefficiency." Local councils sometimes appear overorganized, with countless committees, subcommittees, and steering committees of subcommittees. Loosely related departments which were once separate agencies and which still covet their independence may conflict with one another. One or more of the original constituting agencies likely has a disproportionate share of financial reserves and a historical standing in the community. This too may lead to strains in the organizational life of local councils.

B. PERFORMANCE OF NECESSARY FUNCTIONS. Another factor related to co-ordination is the performance of necessary functions, which isolated churches cannot possibly carry out in any effective or efficient way. These functions have been assumed gradually by councils or granted to them by local churches. Evangelism, religious education, comity, social service, and international relations constitute the typical functions of councils. Some of these activities may be quite extensive and involve many volunteer lay people.

For our purposes it is not necessary to describe in detail each of the functions performed by the various departments of a local council. We must note, however, that new functions have been added—functions which are related to social changes.

Newer council responsibilities include radio and TV broadcasting—particularly, but not solely, in the larger metropolitan councils—hospital chaplaincy, research and survey, work with courts and probation officers, and church directory and publications, among other things. These new functions partly reflect changes in the social structure. The revolution in mass communications, earlier reviewed, has had repercussions on the work of local councils, as local churches, working through the council, seek to take advantage of the newer channels for communicating the faith. In the field of research and survey a new situation exists with the acceptance and emergence of a professional group of church researchers, seeking to apply survey techniques to study churches and communities.[13] Not only is there widespread acceptance of sociological tools for survey, but experience reveals that community surveys done by a council are less expensive and more manageable. After an area has been surveyed by three or four different religious groups, the residents will understandably refuse to co-operate on the fifth query. Church directories and various types of handbooks, published by local councils, respond to the need for information, in view of the complexities of organizational life in a community. The handbooks typically contain resources for referral agencies, including psychiatric clinics, family counseling, adoption services, homes for the aged, and other references within the enlarged scope of the present-day minister's functions.

Perhaps the one activity through which a large group of citizens have annual contact with local councils is the traditional Easter sunrise service. Special occasions and events—such as

[13] In the "Introduction" to the "swan song" of the Institute of Social and Religious Studies, H. Paul Douglass ruefully laments the fact that church researchers are viewed with such suspicion and enjoy so little co-operation from a misunderstanding church public. Cf. H. Paul Douglass, *The Protestant Church as a Social Institution* (New York: Harper & Brothers, 1935).

Easter, Holy-Week Services, Brotherhood Week, Reformation Sunday, United Nations Week, and other special observances comprise the bailiwick of the local conciliar movement. In the observance of these special events, councils play a symbolic role of uniting Protestants in relation to the outside community.

In large measure the functions performed by local councils, signaling increased institutional interdependence, have called councils into being. A local council may begin with voluntary leaders representing clergymen and laymen from various churches in the community. After the functions increase in size and scope, a part-time or full-time executive is sought. Then frequently the number of executives, office staff, and office size will expand. Following a period of organizational stability, the executive may then "move on" and be called to a council in a slightly larger community. Even with the addition of professional personnel, however, local councils must lean heavily on lay leadership and support.

The pattern of assuming necessary functions is not without its elements of institutional strain and stress. Consider the danger that if councils of churches assume only such limited functions as are granted by denominations, council leaders may find themselves relegated to the status of "ecclesiastical errand boys." Particularly in the less well-established councils, executives find themselves frantically engaged in "doing what no one else wants to do." Such a situation imposes role conflicts and inordinate time demands on the council staff. A few denominational executives are beginning to recognize the institutional strains created by council-denominational relationships. Truman B. Douglass of the United Church of Christ has called for a "radical reappraisal" of denominational obligations and an adjustment of their understanding to the real dimensions and significance of the conciliar movement.[14] Some alert laymen are also keenly aware of the organizational stresses in the developing conciliar movement.

[14] "Our Co-operative Witness to Our Oneness in Christ," *Christian Century* (January 8, 1958), 41.

C. ASSIMILATION TO A COMMON CULTURE. Another social factor for the rise of the conciliar movement may be identified as its assimilation to an emerging common culture. As early as 1930, when the movement was in its infancy, H. Paul Douglass predicted that "further federation must wait on assimilation." [15] Assimilation has occurred both in terms of orientation to a common-core Protestantism and to a common-core culture.

Local co-operation in councils is encouraged by the growth of mutual trust and common identity, by the diminution of "social distance" among the various groups. The mutual sharing of common-core Protestantism facilitates this process. Douglass was perhaps a bit extreme when he characterized councils as "the expression of like-mindedness . . . an organization which excludes the unlike and includes the like." [16] Although this opinion contains some truth, frequently one finds more inclusiveness at the local than at the National Council level. In numerous communities, Unitarians, Universalists, Assemblies of God, and Nazarenes have bona fide membership status; and in some local councils Missouri Synod Lutherans and Southern Baptists are active. Orientation to the local community and to a common culture facilitates interchurch relationships. The unifying consequences of an assimilation process led H. Paul Douglass to conclude:

Assimilation has, if not legally the last word, at least the actually determining word in cooperation. . . . It is safe to assume that any future extension of organizational cooperation must be conditioned upon the still more compelling sweep of assimilating processes which shall align together groups now excluded, when they have undergone some modification in their culture and consequent change in their feelings.[17]

In addition, cultural assimilation has led ethnic and racial

[15] *Protestant Cooperation in American Cities*, p. 277.
[16] *Ibid.*
[17] *Ibid.*

groups out of their isolation and into co-operative relationships with other church bodies. With the leveling of social differences, expressions of church unity are encouraged. Negro churches, which in many metropolitan areas constitute the numerical backbone of Protestantism, as whites depart in droves to suburbs, have begun to participate in council affairs.[18] A dramatic instance of this is the election of a Negro Baptist minister to the presidency of the Protestant Council of the City of New York.

In the Flint, Michigan, Council of Churches, the majority of the city's Negro churches are council members; the Church of God, Anderson, Indiana—after being in Flint for twenty-five years—is now seeking full membership status in the council. Similarly, the Buffalo Council of Churches includes churches of the African Methodist Episcopal, African Methodist Episcopal Zion, Evangelical Covenant, Polish National Catholic, Universalist, Unitarian, Ukrainian Christian, Salvation Army, and community churches. A feature editorial study of the Buffalo Council by the *Christian Century* concluded: "Today, when the council speaks, it speaks for Buffalo Protestants . . . but it was not always so." [19]

D. CULTURAL VALUES. Local councils appeal to cultural values in their public relations. "Efficiency" and "economy" have already been treated implicitly. In an earlier connection we noted that these values occupy a prominent place in the constellation of American value themes. Since the average American highly favors "getting things done cheaper, faster, and better," he readily understands the slogan, "do better together than separately," which forms part of the operating definition of the conciliar movement. In its appeal to economy and efficiency, the local council reflects the pragmatic temperament of the American scene.

Such frequently employed terms as "co-operation," "together-

[18] Cf. Robert Lee and Ralph Roy, "The Negro Church," *Christian Century* (October 30, 1957).
[19] The Editors, "Christian Cooperation in Buffalo: A Study of a Successful Council of Churches," *Christian Century* (June 13, 1951).

140

ness," and "unity" suggest another cluster of values. It is an unusual piece of publicity material emanating from council offices which fails to contain one or a combination of several of these values. All three terms are sometimes utilized in urging support for joint efforts to combat the evils of modern society, lest the churches' voice be muffled. "A united voice to speak to the conscience of the community," echoes a typical slogan. The manual for the local conciliar movement is entitled, *Growing Together. Together* is the title of a National Council brochure interpreting the conciliar movement. Councils accentuate religious team-work, much after the analogy of the chain store, which consolidates its efforts in order to render better services.

Other slogans of local councils which convey values are: "That they may be one," "Your Church and mine together—a tower of strength for Unity," and "This City Under God," patterned after the national motto, "This Nation Under God."

While many cultural sources of support undergird these values which are relevant to the conciliar movement, one such source springs from the occupational roles and expectations of council leaders. Laymen whose various vocational roles lead them to see the soundness of such values as efficiency, economy, co-operation, and unity tend to import these same values into the committees and organizational structures of the conciliar movement. A businessman whose work-a-day world may be caught up in promoting such values or a doctor who co-operates in a community hospital or clinic and whose work gains reinforcement by membership in the city, county, and national medical associations— these and other lay leaders bring to the boards and committees of councils cultural values which buttress the work of the conciliar movement.

E. URBANIZATION. Local councils share more or less the same concern earlier noted in the founding of the Federal Council; namely, the concern that Protestantism make an impact in confronting the evils of modern society. And cities are often the place where social evils are centered in dramatic and alarming ways. In our accounting, the urban community is the final social source of the rise of the local conciliar movement. An analysis of the distribution of councils reveals the arresting picture of a direct relationship between size of city and existence of a council. In a sense, councils of churches are a function of the size of a community. Of the nearly 4,300 cities in the United States, 106 are classified as "largest cities" (defined by the Census Bureau as having a population of 101,000 or more).[20] An examination of these "largest cities" shows the striking pattern that all but ten have a council of churches.

The ten cities without a council are all located in the South. Therefore, 90 per cent of the so-called "largest cities" have councils, and if the South were excluded, the figure would run 100 per cent. Although rapid strides have been made in recent years, the conciliar movement in the South remains relatively underdeveloped. It should be noted, however, that size of cities bears some influence even in the Southern scene. The first thirteen largest Southern cities, ranging in population from 594,321 (Houston, Texas) to 203,404 (Jacksonville, Florida) do have councils of churches.

Several hypotheses may be advanced with respect to the conciliar movement in the South: (1) The South is less urban than other sections of the country. The 1950 United States Census reports 47 per cent urbanization in the South, as compared to 64 per cent for the nation as a whole. (2) Certain large groups, notably the Southern Baptist Convention, dominate the religious situation. This suggests the hypothesis that the more diffused the church membership, the greater likelihood that there will be a council of churches. We might predict that in cities where Protestantism is dominated by a few denominations the demand for a council will not be keen; or, if one exists, it will likely be a *pro forma* organization. As an explanation for this, recalling our earlier discussion in this chapter, in such cities less urgency exists for functional co-ordination. In the eyes

[20] In 1850 there were only six cities in the United States with 101,000 population or over, and by 1900 there were thirty-eight cities of this size.

of dominant religious groups who wield the power in the religious life of the community the need for co-operation is less pronounced. Hence local councils may be viewed as an institutional response to a religious situation of competition and potential conflict in a community in view of its religious heterogeneity. (3) A third hypothesis for the relative paucity of councils in the South concerns the race factor. Many local councils in the South—such as Atlanta, New Orleans, Louisville ,and Lexington—are interracial. Since councils tend to express and reflect local community values, numerous Southern communities will resist organizations with interracial participation and program. Moreover, in the public mind, local councils may be associated with the National Council of Churches, whose vigorous policy of a "nonsegregated church in a nonsegregated society" is not shared in the bulk of Southern communities.

Having examined the deviancy of the South, we are ready to return to the original observation that the existence of a council depends largely on a community's size. The larger the city, the more developed and organizationally complex its council of churches. With decreased population size the proportion of cities with councils diminishes rapidly. All cities with over one million population have a council with a large executive staff, with some councils numbering over twenty in professional personnel.

Of the ninety-six "largest cities" in the United States with councils, eighty-nine of them have an employed staff, whereas seven—chiefly newly created councils—have a volunteer staff. Regardless of its location, every city with a population of 200,000 contains a council of churches. This finding has practical significance for churchmen in expanding communities which are approaching the 200,000 population size. Such communities where a council does not now exist may well profit by planning in advance.

This affinity between size of city on the one hand and the existence and strength of councils on the other gives rise to additional implications. In smaller communities, councils of churches are more difficult to sustain and their survival more precarious; their leadership and financial base are more tenuous. Moreover, the demand for co-ordination and performance of specialized services is less marked. Organizational complexity and the potentialities of interchurch conflict and strain are correspondingly diminished. In large urban centers and metropolitan areas, however, this situation does not obtain. One finds organizations of every type elaborated in complex forms. Increased compartmentalization, segmentation, and specialization of institutions call forth agencies of co-ordination. For the more complex the social setting, the less effective an individual voice, and the greater the potentialities for interchurch strain and conflict. In these larger urban places, councils of churches constitute a necessary, national pattern of interchurch co-operation and mediate interchurch tensions which may be latent.

Urbanization in this country has increased markedly, so that the urban to rural proportion today stands at 65 per cent to 35 per cent.[21] This proportion represents nearly the exact reversal of the urban-rural ratio at the turn of the century. With the rise of urbanization and the new social relationships it imposes, the growth and development of councils has kept pace. As the urban trend continues, one may expect the continued expansion of the local conciliar movement. The fact that councils are associated with large urban centers in amount and intensity suggests their concomitance with large-scale organizational life, which is a mark of contemporary American society. Thus one of the social sources of the conciliar movement is the emergence and ascendance of urbanization in the United States.

IV. SUMMARY

This chapter traced the rise of the conciliar movement in its national and local forms. It noted the interdependent re-

[21] In the Middle Atlantic and New England states, where councils exist in greater quantity, over 86 per cent of the population live in urban areas, whereas the figure for the South, as previously noted, is considerably lower.

lationships between these two rational structures for co-operative Protestantism. Social factors have played an explicit and implicit role in the development and intensification of the movement. Particularly noteworthy were functions performed by councils—functions which are most effectively handled when located in a co-ordinating body of nation-wide or community-wide scope, as the case may be. Corporate expression was also vital in confronting social issues and expressing political action, in dealing with community and national public and private agencies, in symbolically confronting the non-Protestant Roman Catholic and secular community. The conciliar movement also responds to the challenge of community social changes, of the increased interdependence of American society, and of the rising tide of urbanization. The assimilation process and various cultural values play a supportive role in the maintenance of the conciliar movement.

Our next chapter deals with local, community-centered churches—another expression of co-operative Protestantism.

6. Local Community-Centered Churches

The expression of church unity at the local level in the form of community-centered churches is another familiar feature of American Protestantism. As early as 1928 David R. Piper referred to the development of community churches as the "most significant present-day church movement in America." He noted their expansion from a few scattered churches in 1917 to more than 1,296 by 1927—an increase of over 1,100 per cent.

When we consider that even on this conservative estimate there are more community churches than there are Friends churches of all kinds in America, and more than the total number of Unitarian and Universalist churches combined, we see that, considered as a group, the community churches are beginning to take no mean place in the religious life of America. When again we note the growth of the movement . . . we perceive here a movement which has none of the marks of the ephemeral, and which represents therefore a steadily growing conviction concerning religious organization.[1]

Local community-centered churches reveal a pattern of baffling complexity and variety. Indeed, the designation "local community-centered churches" sounds a bit awkward.[2] It in-

[1] *Community Churches* (New York: Harper & Brothers). Used by permission.
[2] This term is used so as to distinguish the data for analysis from the movement known as "Council of Community Churches," formerly called International Council of Community Churches," and before that "Community Church Workers

tends to refer to those forms of unity and co-operation taking place at the local parish neighborhood level, where the day-to-day religious institutional life is lived. Typical references are, "federated church," "united church," "union church," "community church," "larger parish," "interdenominational church," "nondenominational church," "undenominational church," "neighorhood church," "yoked parish."

The problem would be simpler if one could say that community-centered churches lack a denominational tie. Such is not the case, however, for many so-called "community churches" have one or more denominational relationships. Moreover, innumerable denominational churches behave like community churches, particularly those churches organized by comity arrangement.

Let us note at the outset that community-centered churches are not uniformly accepted as authentic ecclesiastical structures. At the Oberlin Conference on Faith and Order one prominent church official called them "ecclesiastical monstrosities." They have been thought of as "without father, without mother, and without descent."

Although no one has taken a count of the precise number of community-centered churches—the figures vary from two thousand to six thousand—all would agree that such an identifiable institution exists on the American religious scene. In fact, H. Paul Douglass observed that if these churches were combined into one separate denomination, they would constitute one of the major American church bodies.[3]

I. TYPES OF COMMUNITY-CENTERED CHURCHES

Four types of community-centered churches are discernible: (1) independent community church, (2) affiliated community

---

of America." Our focus is more comprehensive than that embodied in this movement.

[3] "Ecumenicity in America," *Toward World-Wide Christianity*, p. 184.

church, (3) denominational community church, (4) federated community church.

1. The independent community church. As its name implies, this type of church is unrelated to any denominational or ecclesiastical source. Frequently the independent community church organizes self-consciously as a compromise or a reaction against denominationalism. Sometimes it is militantly antidenominational, as was the Community Church of Great Neck, Long Island, at its inception.

In small communities, what were once denominational churches may decide to give up the futile struggle for existence and discard all the marks of denominational connections. Thus in Castile, New York, five denominations, each striving to serve the less than one thousand Protestants in the community, joined to form the United Community Church. Denominational ties were completely severed. In succeeding years, the church has been served by a Lutheran, a Presbyterian, a Congregationalist, and an Evangelical and Reformed minister. Now a strong church is possible where several weak ones competing with one another previously existed.

In spite of its advantages, such a system contains weaknesses, since no central place exists for drawing its supply of ministers. There remain such problems as ministerial pensions, literature and curricular materials, channeling of benevolent funds for home and foreign missions. Many earlier churches of this type either failed to collect such funds or else their giving was slight. Some independent community churches deviate from the main stream of Protestantism, taking on the character of pan-Protestant centers for religion in general.

Lacking denominational ties, independent community churches frequently request sponsorship from the local council of churches.

The movement known as the "Council of Community Churches" generally—though not exclusively—represents churches of the independent community type. Said one of its leaders:

Many of our churches are unions of two or more congregations which dropped their ecclesiastical relationships when they united. . . . Some were denominational churches but dropped their connection in the hopes of a wider appeal within their communities or from discontent.[4]

The council is a voluntary association of independent, autonomous community churches. It represents the merger of a Negro and a white community church movement. Known as the Biennial Council of Community Churches, the Negro group joined with the National Council of Community Churches in 1950. At present the membership is about evenly balanced between Negroes and whites; by tacit agreement, the organization's presidency rotates annually between a Negro and a white leader. Current membership runs between two and three hundred local churches. Total membership tends to fluctuate, since churches must renew their affiliation annually. Apparently, however, enthusiasm for this form of community-centered church has been waning since its high point in the 1920's. In 1929 some 1,200 community churches were registered with the office of the Community Church Workers of America.

Whether the Council of Community Churches constitutes another denomination brings up a moot point. Council leaders insist on a negative answer and indicate that careful precautions are taken against such institutionalization. Thus Roy Burkhart claims that the "unique fact about the community church movement is that it is the only religious institution bearing the name of church that has successfully resisted the temptation to become another denomination." [5] Nevertheless, the reiterations of the Council's leaders have not convinced the general church public. For the Council performs many of the co-ordinating and advisory functions commonly associated with a denominational headquarters.

True, the Council does not ordain its own ministers; but

[4] Willis E. Elliott, "Unity Through Community," *Christian Century* (May 8, 1957).
[5] "The Community Church," *Christendom,* XI (Spring, 1946), 188.

149

it has a formal constitution, assists in placement of clergy, conducts an "annual conference," and publishes a "house organ," *The Christian Community.* Represented by delegations at various ecumenical gatherings, the organization also enjoys membership in numerous local councils of churches.

Perhaps the leaders of the Council of Community Churches are overly sensitive about the charge of being another denomination. In the organizational context of American culture, one should not be surprised if community churches evolve in the denominational pattern, and denominational churches drift in the direction of community churches.

One thing about the Council of Community Churches appears certain: as an organization, it has effectively bridged racial and class lines and is fully integrated. In a sense the Council illustrates our central thesis. It has successfully merged a Negro and a white group which have by no means been on an economic and social parity. The reduction and the overcoming of these social differences enable social integration and religious unity, which is favored with the erosion of racial and class differences.

2. The affiliated community church. The affiliated community church is a modification of the independent type by having an "attenuated connection" with one or several denominations. Such loose affiliation with denominations provides open channels for ministerial supply and for distribution of benevolences. At the same time, it preserves the values of a community-oriented church relatively free from denominational obligations.

Affiliated churches form in numerous ways. Some develop out of former independent parishes in view of insurmountable difficulties faced in finding ministerial supply. Others affiliate in order to receive missionary aid from a denomination. In a few cases affiliation is sought for the sake of protection from invasion by competing denominational groups. Some churches originate as affiliated congregations. Several well-known parishes have followed this pattern. The Riverside Church in New York City began as a church with an undenominational tendency, although affiliated with the American Baptist Convention. Later it also affiliated with the New York City Congregational Church Association and has reflected a conscious choice to be interdenominational, as it continues to explore affiliation with other denominations.

Park Forest United Protestant Church has become widely known through William H. Whyte's analysis of it in *The Organization Man.*[6] In view of the diversity of denominational backgrounds represented among the "uprooted suburbanites" of Park Forest, Whyte observes that the young families desired "a true union of the leading Protestant denominations, not a community church of the older type."[7]

Another well-known, pioneer expression of an interdenominational approach to the community is the East Harlem Protestant Parish. Its ministry, which one urban church student calls "radical experimentation,"[8] serves a neglected people and a depressed neighborhood, inhabited largely by Puerto Ricans, Negroes, and Italians. The community's social disorganization served as an inducement for the young instigators of the work to attack, as "ecumenicity does battle in the front-line trenches."[9] Thus social factors, in some measure, provided the impetus for a unitive church response.

The Parish began as a store-front church in 1948 and soon expanded to include other store fronts and a church building. One of the parishes, the Church of the Ascension, is affiliated with the Presbyterian Church, U.S.A. East Harlem Protestant Parish receives support and direction from eight national denominational boards, in addition to the New York City Mission Society, Union Theological Seminary, and the Home Missions Division of the National Council of Churches. Members of the Parish's "group ministry" include ordained ministers from

[6] New York: Simon and Schuster, 1956, pp. 365-81.
[7] *Ibid.*, p. 369.
[8] Ross W. Sanderson, *The Church Serves the Changing City* (New York: Harper & Brothers, 1955), pp. 190-231.
[9] *Ibid.*, p. 213.

seven religious bodies. Growing out of East Harlem's trail-blazing experiment, inner city Protestant parishes have spread to other urban centers, including New Haven, Chicago, and Cleveland.

3. The denominational community church. Denominational community churches serve their community in a comprehensive way, sometimes in behalf of all the churches, and yet maintain complete fellowship in their own denominations. Increasingly these churches are commissioned to serve the entire Protestant constituency through an assignment by comity. Such churches may also be formed through a consolidation of two or more churches which retain but one denominational loyalty. Often these mergers occur between two local churches of the same communion, or two groups whose parent bodies have united.

Of course the dividing line between an affiliated community church and a denominational one is rather ill-defined; for it frequently becomes impossible to discern precisely where affiliation stops and connection begins. Some affiliated churches drift into full denominational status.

Denominational community churches may retain the denomination's name, like the "Community Presbyterian Church of Lomita" (California). Sometimes it appears in parentheses, as "Garden City Community Church (Congregational)." At any rate, the designation "community" tends to be featured. Perhaps it signals the doubtful asset of a denominational label for appealing to new residents in the community, lest support be granted only by those stemming from a particular denominational background. Particularly is this the case with lesser known and perhaps less respected denominations, whose past may be tainted by an ethnic stigma of foreignness. Hence the "community" label tends to neutralize previous associations, social and religious differences. Such practice reflects assimilation to a common-core Protestantism and a common-core culture.

Countless new communities, profiting from past mistakes of overchurching, have established denominational community churches. The comity process which fosters this practice will occupy our attention at a later stage.

4. The federated community church. Our fourth type, the federated community church, springs from the merger of two or more churches of different denominational backgrounds who desire to maintain their loyalties to the several denominations represented. While the component committees of a federated church stand separate, they function together as one unit. Hence both parties retain their own membership rolls, boards of trustees and deacons, property rights, and benevolences. But they act as one in calling and paying a minister, in worship services, and in local social and civic affairs involving the federated church.

This pattern of local interchurch co-operation enables parishes to preserve their denominational identity while uniting the efforts of diverse religious groups in the community. It is a typical institutional response in numerous American villages which are faced with the social situation of declining population. Economic pressures thus force many churches to federate, as Dean Willard L. Sperry noted:

Many American villages are badly over-churched. Each little loyal group taxes itself beyond its resources to maintain its corporate life, but the time comes when further independent survival is economically impossible. The villagers are all neighbors; they meet at their work; they pass the time of day at the post office and in the general store. They have no need to be introduced and interpreted to one another. . . . They finally agree to federate. There are no serious theological hurdles to be negotiated, only a few stubborn habits to be accommodated to one another. Thus a fisherman on an island off the coast of Maine confronted with the proposal that his church join its neighbor over the way said, "Wa-a-ll, I don't know whether we kin do thet or not. They sing three hymns, and we sing only two!" [10]

[10] *Religion in America* (New York: Cambridge University Press). Used by permission.

Laymen often prefer the federated pattern, because it makes the smallest demands and yet affords a large amount of co-operation in the local setting. The parties which federate suffer no loss in property, tradition, or denominational loyalty; yet each is strengthened by the new fellowship. One minister can be given an adequate salary to perform the tasks of several poorly paid ones. At the same time many laymen regard it as advantageous that under the federated system one of the parties may "pull out" if the need should arise, since the churches are not organically united.

While amalgamation or dissolution of the relationship sometimes happens, some federated churches remain permanently so related. Such is the case particularly for "larger parishes"— a device for federating separate parishes fairly well scattered in open-country, rural areas.

Federated community churches are by no means confined to the rural setting. In mid-town Manhattan a plan is currently under way to federate the efforts of five churches into a "United West Side Parish." A Congregational, Evangelical and Reformed, Evangelical United Brethren, and two Presbyterian churches are represented in this endeavor to bring a total Protestant ministry to the changed neighborhood.

II. ROLE OF SOCIAL FACTORS

From the foregoing discussion of four types of community-centered churches, we may lift up several implications bearing on the role of social factors. Many observers of church unity in America regard the development of community-centered churches as the clearest indication of the social sources of unity. For on the local level, the divisive and damaging effects of excessive denominational competition are dramatically visible. Now we shall examine the role of social factors as they encourage community-centered churches.

A. COMMUNITIES WITH DECLINING POPULATION. Population changes—either of decline or growth—

play a prominent part. Consider first the problem of declining population. Neighborhoods undergoing sudden shifts in racial, cultural, ethnic, or socio-economic composition have come to be known as the "grave yard of Protestant churches." The churches' reaction has been traditionally dictated by flight and fear as they fled from transitional neighborhoods by moving "uptown" or to suburban areas. There is ample evidence, however, that churches in areas of social change are not taking flight, but increasingly seeking ways to serve the changed community.

One of the chief alternatives is to develop a common strategy in co-operation with neighboring churches. Such strategy frequently takes the form of merger, consolidation, or federation. The "First Federated Church, Presbyterian and Reformed" of Bayonne, New Jersey, furnishes an example of this course of action. Bayonne was formerly an exclusive summer resort of vacationing New Yorkers. Today it has become an industrial community, with fumes from the gas and oil refineries permeating the atmosphere. Although the total population numbers around 75,000, only about 5,000 are Protestant. Yet, in 1950, twenty-eight Protestant churches struggled for survival. Average attendance of these congregations numbered eighty-six persons. Competition for the available Protestant population was keen. In 1952, three of the churches—Christ Presbyterian, First, and the Third Reformed Churches—united to form the First Federated Church, Presbyterian and Reformed. The social pressures which stand behind the merger of these three churches are painfully clear. Dwindling membership, the high cost of maintenance, and costly competition force churches to seek new and viable institutional patterns of adaptation if they wish to survive in the changed community.

Similar accounts may be duplicated in numerous urban places across the nation. For a transitional community cannot long endure the sheer costliness of maintaining institutions for little more than the sake of preserving traditional ties and loyalties. Samuel C. Kincheloe, pioneer urban church researcher, formerly of Chicago Theological Seminary, has pointed to the necessity of institutional adjustment, lest churches face what he picturesquely termed, "the behavior sequence of a dying church." Kincheloe concluded:

In areas of transition where once there was a prosperous Protestant community, churches may federate. These areas may have been over-churched in the beginning. Just as soon as a number of the attendants and supporters of these churches move away, it becomes patent that there are too many churches in the community. It is natural, therefore, for these Protestant churches in their efforts to live, to federate.[11]

Although merger and relocation are not the only alternatives facing churches in changing communities, students of church life have learned one practical lesson: in order to be effective, if not for the sake of survival, the local church must serve its changing community; and in adapting to the needs of the new community the church becomes community-centered in orientation, ready to unite all those living in a given community into one fellowship.

Mergers and federations of churches in changed communities often result in a new lease of life. This is particularly true for churches which are no longer self-supporting. From the practical standpoint, the greater effectiveness of a co-operative or interdenominational approach springs, not from the presence or absence of a certain confessional witness, but from the fact that the financial burden is too great for any one group to bear alone. In addition, the removal from the field of one or more religious groups in an overchurched community means that competition is reduced and resources may be deployed in other areas of need and merit.

In rural communities population shifts also impinge upon the institutional life of the church. Traditionally, urban populations cannot reproduce themselves, but derive their growth

[11] "Major Reactions of City Churches," *Religious Education* (November, 1928), 5.

from the steady supply of rural in-migrants.[12] Replenishment of urban areas frequently results in depletion of rural communities. With declining constituencies, many rural churches are left struggling for survival. In order to retain the services of trained leadership or to eliminate the waste of competitive rivalry, rural parishes may resort to federation or merger.

One institutional device employed by churches in sparsely settled areas is the "larger parish" system. In many respects this form of organization resembles the consolidation of rural school districts. The larger parish plan represents a federation of a group of churches in a given area.[13] It enables a pooling of leadership and a reduction of the spirit of competition through mutual sharing and support. Through mergers, federations, or larger parishes, so-called "marginal churches" are provided with adequate ministries.

A Case Study. It may be instructive for our purpose of indicating the role of social factors to cite briefly a case study of a local church currently in the process of adaptation to a changed neighborhood.[14] Called Evangelical Church and located in Brooklyn Heights this parish has been subject to two different— though related—types of adaptation, which we shall label internal and external adjustment.

Internal adjustment began almost with the founding of the church in 1841 as the "German Evangelical United Church in Brooklyn," on the corner of Cranberry and Fulton Streets. In 1844 the congregation moved to its present location on Schermerhorn Street. With the move came a change in the

[12] At one time this generalization was an established fact of urban sociology. Since World War II, however, urban net reproduction rates experienced a sharp increase, and urban families of four and five children are not uncommon. Whether this shift in values, which some attribute to an economy of abundance, will continue remains to be seen.

[13] Cf. Edmund S. Brunner, *The Larger Parish* (New York: Institute of Social and Religious Research, 1934), p. 7; Marvin Judy, *The Larger Parish and Group Ministry* (Nashville: Abingdon Press, 1959).

[14] For a detailed survey of the problem of adaptation in a changing community cf. Robert Lee, *Protestant Churches in the Brooklyn Heights* (New York: Brooklyn Division of the Protestant Council of the City of New York), 1954.

church's name to "Deutsche Evangelische Kirche." Note that
the congregation shifted from an English to a German orientation. Recall also that this was a period of successive waves of
German in-migration. Hence internal adjustments were made
in the church to accommodate the newcomers. Membership
grew to such an extent that by 1888 the congregation erected
a new edifice with a seating capacity of one thousand on the
same site. Historical records indicate that the years 1886 to
1930 were the "most glorious years" in the life of the parish.
Up to 1930 the German language was spoken exclusively.
Then after 1930 two separate services were held—one conducted in German, the other in English. This practice prevailed until World War II. With the onset of the war the German language was dropped entirely. Moreover, the name of the
church was again changed. This time the ethnic label was discarded, and the church took on the name of its street, "Schermerhorn Street Evangelical Church" or, in its shortened form
today, "Evangelical Church." This change in name reflected
greater assimilation to American culture, drifting away of the
earlier German constituency, and, most significantly, the feeling that a German name was un-American. For it expressed
the taint of foreignness and constituted a source of embarrass-
ment during the war years. Although this effect was only
slightly felt during World War I, its full force was experienced
during World War II.

Coupled with these internal adjustments were crucial external adjustments confronting the church. The once quiet
and prosperous residential neighborhood was undergoing meta-
morphosis. Its residents increasingly took flight to the suburbs
and were replaced by new, younger families, and particularly
by Puerto Rican newcomers. The area adjacent to the church
soon fell into a stage of transition, with relatively complete
displacement by the Puerto Ricans. Across the way stands a
Spanish-speaking movie house. A few doors down, on the corner,
a vender sells Spanish-language newspapers and magazines.
Nearly every store in the immediate vicinity employs or is

operated by Spanish-speaking folk. Across the street is a Greek Orthodox Church. Not far around the block one comes upon the headquarters of the "Islamic Mission of America for the Propagation of Islam." This has indeed turned into a polyglot neighborhood. What a vast difference, the pastor wistfully observed, from the days when he went around the neighborhood from door to door greeting his parishioners. Today, not one single parishioner lives within a half mile of the Evangelical Church! Family homes have been cut up for multiple dwelling units. Others have been razed to make room for private and government office buildings. The church now finds itself "downtown."

How has the church weathered these vast internal and external changes? It has obviously "gone down-hill." About two hundred members remain, but only some fifty or seventy-five attend worship services on Sunday, for the most part traveling in from the suburbs. A men's club, young adult program, and youth group have all disbanded since World War II. Now taught entirely in English, the Sunday school has gradually dwindled, until some thirty-odd remain. In 1951, one of the members wrote a poem to commemorate the Church's centennial. It shows, as only poetry can portray, the affection for the church and a sadness over the inevitability of its fate:

We thank Thee that, when beaten or discouraged
By earthly cares that seem to grow each day,
When vanquished in the halls of law or commerce,
Our Church remains, a few short steps away.

A symbol of the Faith that lives forever.
A Church that has endured through peace and war,
Has seen a century of sudden changes
And stays unchanged and tranquil as before.

The City has pressed ever closer 'round us,
A turbulent and ever restless sea;

159

God grant our Church remain through change and tumult
A still, calm island of eternity.[15]

The paradoxical truth conveyed in these poetic lines is that
the Evangelical Church has become, in fact, a cultural island
amidst a sea of new people and strange buildings. As to the
future, plans are being discussed to move to a new neighborhood or to merge with another church. Clearly the alternative
is to move or to merge, since the present church program lacks
viability to serve the community's newcomers. Either relocation
or merger, in any case, would completely transform and disrupt
earlier church patterns, minimizing further its original ethnic
base and appeal.

Social factors impinging upon the fortunes of this church
and common to many other churches in changing communities,
include, extinction of foreign language, suburban flight of parishioners, new ethnic groups, changing patterns of land use
and housing, different age levels, and the economic decline of
the neighborhood. Under such social pressures, a united Protestant witness is the most effective means of communicating the
Christian faith.

B. COMMUNITIES WITH EXPANDING POPULA-
TION. Community-centered churches develop not only in response to dwindling or shifting population in urban and rural
areas, but are also prominent features of communities experi-
encing rapid growth. New suburban developments, war-born industrial communities, and government research centers provide
fertile soil for experiments in local community-centered
churches. To a considerable extent, these churches are born of
necessity in areas of declining population. But in newer areas of
population growth, many community churches emerge out of
the self-conscious desire of the new residents; such desire is
frequently supported by denominational officials for the sake
of planning and developing churches in an orderly fashion.

[15] Marie C. Lafrenz, "Sanctuary," *One Hundred Years of Christian Service*
(New York: Evangelical Church, 1951). Used by permission.

Although no comparative statistics have been gathered, church officials responsible for church extension generally surmise that the growth of community-centered churches is greatest in the West Coast—in such states as California, Washington, and Oregon. This observation tends to fit the generalization regarding areas of rapid population growth and expansion, for the Pacific Coast is the most rapidly growing region in the nation.

In addition to the trend of westward migration, consider the mobility to the suburbs. The rise of suburbia, chiefly in the last three decades, has been noted as one of the social revolutions of our day. Suburban population increased 210 per cent, while the nation as a whole went up only 64 per cent in the last forty years. Today suburbia is the home of some 42,500,000 Americans. Many commentators have pointed to the patterns of conformity and social homogeneity encouraged by suburban life.[16] Sylvia Fava suggests a high degree of primary-group-relatedness or "neighboring" in suburban communities. The new "mass-produced suburbs" have a way of melting down religious differences and denominational lines. Church affiliation in Park Forest or Crestwood Heights more likely follows the traffic flow than denominational channels. William Whyte contends that the high rate of mobility actually weakens the denominational allegiances of Park Foresters:

Their mobility, far from making them cling to a single church

[16] Sylvia Fava, "Suburbanism as a Way of Life," *American Sociological Review*, XXI (February, 1956); Waldo Beach, "Euphoria in Suburbia," *Christianity and Crisis* (April 2, 1956); William Whyte, "The Outgoing Life," *Fortune* (July, 1953); Harry Henderson, "The Mass Produced Suburbs," *Harper's Magazine*, 207 (November, 1953), 25-32; Kenneth Miller, "Our Growing Suburbs and Their Churches," *Religion in Life* (Autumn, 1955); Hugo Leinberger, "The Church in the 'New Suburb,'" *Religious Education* (January-February, 1955); Gibson Winter, "The Church in Suburban Captivity," *Christian Century* (September 28, 1955); John Seeley, R. A. Sims, E. W. Loosley, *Crestwood Heights: A Study of the Culture of Suburban Life* (New York: Basic Books, Inc., 1956.) Although the literature depicting the "outgoing life" in "mass produced" suburbs leaves the impression of cultural homogeneity, it must be recalled there are various types of suburbs, including industrial suburbs where social life and prestige patterns are not so distinct.

affiliation as a sort of constant in their lives, has weakened the denominational barriers. In moving from one community to another, many of the transients had gone where there was either no church of their faith or one that to them seemed mediocre. . . . Of all the factors that weighed in their choice, denomination had become relatively unimportant. In a house-to-house survey of their religious preferences, Park Foresters were asked . . . what counted most to them in choosing a church. Here, in order, are the factors they listed: (1) the minister, (2) the Sunday school, (3) the location. In fourth and fifth places, the denomination and the music.[17]

An indigenous spirit of independence and self-determination seems to mark the establishment of community-centered churches in new suburban developments. The high degree of neighboring and the quest for a place to belong, in view of the rootlessness of highly mobile suburban families, fosters this sense of self-determination in starting new churches. Whyte highlights the fusion of an independent pioneering spirit with an orientation of "community togetherness" as ingredients in the formation of Park Forest's United Protestant Churches.

Still another example of community self-determination, together with joint planning by eleven denominations, is the experience of the community-centered churches of Richland, Washington. Of interest is the diversity of the co-operating denominations in the Richland "ecumenical experiment." They include Advent-Christian, American Baptist, Disciples of Christ, Evangelical and Reformed, Presbyterian, U.S.A., United Presbyterian, Friends, Church of the Brethren, Evangelical United Brethren, Methodist, and Congregational-Christian.

Richland was a sparsely settled farming community until the United States government decided to establish a large plant to produce atomic bomb materials there. Fifty thousand laborers were suddenly imported into the construction area. As the construction workers completed their job and departed, a new corps of operators, secretaries, engineers, and scientists, with their families, descended upon the community. The denomina-

[17] Whyte, *op. cit.*, pp. 367-68. Used by permission.

tions might well have started a big rush to "get there first with the most." They were not so inclined, however, and the residents would not have it that way in any case. Instead a carefully devised program of joint planning and co-operation was instituted. Today six "United Protestant Churches" serve the Protestant constituency in the Richland vicinity. Each church acts as a community church. But each church is also affiliated with a denomination or with the state council of churches. The Richland lay leaders express their self-determining sentiments, as reflected in the following:

> The rank and file of people in Richland rejoice in seeing denominational barriers broken down and have little but good to say about the United Protestant Churches. In the main, pastoral leadership has been sympathetic to the movement. When the denominational urge in a minister becomes too strong, however, the laymen hold him in line! [18]

One of the consequences of local self-determination is that community-centered churches likely have a multiplicity of denominational backgrounds represented in their fellowship. As earlier intimated in our discussion of interchangeable memberships, for a local church to have thirty or forty different groups within its membership is not uncommon. Thus the church in Radburn, one of the celebrated community-centered churches located in Fair Lawn, New Jersey, contains thirty-four different religious bodies. These include, besides the more familiar groups, Jehovah's Witnesses, Plymouth Brethren, Missouri Synod Lutheran, Scotch Congregational, Society of Friends, Southern Baptists, Universalists, Gospel Tabernacle, and Eastern Orthodox, Jewish, and Roman Catholic. Such diversity in a community-centered church of a fairly orthodox Protestant stripe suggests an ongoing pattern of cultural and religious assimilation which plows the ground for the development of local forms of church unity. Hence the diversity of

---

[18] Clayton S. Rice, "United Protestant Churches," *The City Church* (January-February, 1954) 27-30.

denominational backgrounds in local church memberships provides one of the practical fruits of American ecumenicity at the grassroots level.[19]

C. CULTURAL VALUES. The desire for community-centered churches and the self-determination of local residents to establish them in countless communities cannot be attributed solely to the newness of these communities or to the high degree of neighboring, or even to the mobility of population. Doubtless these social pressures are involved. In addition, as seen in preceding chapters, various cultural values sustain institutional structures. These supportive values play a profound role in the development of community-centered churches.

Chief among these values is efficiency. Many laymen regard community churches as an efficient and sensible way of religious organizational life. They see the waste of valuable resources involved in competition and duplication where communities are overchurched. If citizens can work co-operatively in civic life—in the community chest, in farmers' organizations, and in other voluntary associations—the question arises, "Why can't co-operation be carried over into the life of the churches?" The efficiency motif, earlier noted as one of the major American value themes, finds expression in these sentiments for local church unity by laymen and clergymen:

"One large building for worship can be built and maintained for less than several small ones."

"When all the Protestants of a community come to work together, more real work is done.

"A community church can serve the community in many ways that require salaried workers besides the pastor.

"Many communities that support three or four pastors, janitors, choirs, organists, etc., would get better results if this same money were used to support one pastor, one choir, one organist playing a real organ, one church building adequately cared for, a church

[19] Yoshio Fukuyama, "The Theological Implications of Mobility," *Christian Unity in North America,* ed. J. Robert Nelson (St. Louis: Bethany Press, 1958), p. 201.

secretary to do the work which robs most pastors of time greatly needed, a deaconess, a religious educator, etc." [20]

Desire for efficiency wins overwhelming lay support. Thus one layman contends, "The more co-operation we have, the more efficient we will be. We can't afford to waste the Lord's time and money—this is a sin against the Holy Ghost!" Efficiency provides a strong inducement for favoring and sustaining local community-centered churches.

Another value is activism or participation in community life. Many consider David Riesman's characterization of contemporary American life as "other-directed" to be a particularly fitting description of the social organization of suburbia.[21] Chaplain Hugo Leinberger, who organized the first United Protestant Church in Park Forest, echoes this note of other-directedness when he comments, "In a community like Park Forest, when young people see how many other people are going to church regularly, they feel they ought to." [22] Common participation and identity are present and powerful in many suburbs due to common backgrounds, interests, ages, incomes, and occupations. Such commonality promotes social compatibility and increases participation in community affairs and social activities.

Common participation and interest are also enhanced by the relatively large number of younger families with children in many suburban communities. Solid grounds exist for the view that children draw adults into community participation in voluntary associations.[23] Married couples with children are more likely to join organizations than childless couples. This finding is corroborated by Janowitz, whose study of Chicago

[20] Piper, op. cit., pp. 18 ff. By permission of Harper & Brothers.

[21] David Riesman, Nathan Glazer, and Reul Denney, The Lonely Crowd (New Haven: Yale University Press, 1950). Cf. Whyte, op. cit.; Seeley, Sim, and Loosley, op. cit.; John P. Marquand, "Portrait of a Striver," Outside Readings in Sociology, ed. E. A. Schuler, D. L. Gibson, M. L. Fiero, and W. B. Brookover (New York: Thomas Y. Crowell Company, 1952), pp. 351-59.

[22] Whyte, op. cit., p. 367.

[23] Cf. Wright and Hyman, op. cit., p. 292.

residents concluded: "Children are not only the best neighbors in the community, but they lead their parents to neighborhood community participation and orientation." [24] Expressions of local self-determination and participation in voluntary organizations suggest the articulation of a newly found social cohesiveness at the community level. The very design and physical setting of many suburbs fosters and insures a sense of exclusiveness and tends to heighten internal interaction of the residents.

Dwellers in new suburban communities give special priority to the founding of churches. Such participation often serves as a vehicle for symbolizing the new social status achieved by the suburbanite.[25] The suburban church may well be a prestige-conferring center in the community's life; new social status acquired by moving to the exclusive suburban neighborhood is celebrated by belonging to the church.[26] Membership thus solidifies newly achieved status and gives evidence of the fact that the newcomer belongs. Doubtless these social attitudes which support the unity of the community are carried over in the formation of its churches. Hence local church unity in suburbia is favored by the community's cultural homogeneity.

Local community-centered churches, like the conciliar movement earlier discussed, are very much caught up in the cultural values of American society. Often laymen and clergymen are

[24] *Op. cit.*, p. 124.

[25] Support for the latent status-bearing function of the church is given in a careful empirical analysis of Protestant Episcopal Church parishioners. Cf. Benjamin B. Ringer, "The Parishioner and His Church: A Study in the Sociology of Religion" (unpublished Ph.D. dissertation, Columbia University, 1956), p. 221: "Those who are of *low status* but who desire to move upward—find the church (at least the one under study) an effective vehicle for moving up the social ladder. Its accessibility as an elite institution enables them to satisfy their status aspirations in a 'better' surrounding than would be available to them in a secular community."

[26] The relationship between religious and cultural identification is discussed by Will Herberg, *op. cit.*, and by Stanley Rowland, Jr., "Suburbia Buys Religion," *The Nation* (July 28, 1956). *New York Times* reporter, Rowland wrote: "The main mood of many a suburban church on Sundays is that of a fashionable shopping center. This is cultural identification on a wide, superficial, and generally unacknowledged level. On week-days one shops for food, on Saturdays one shops for recreation, and on Sunday, one shops for the Holy Ghost."

guided by a limited set of values which claim their allegiance. A realistic awareness of this tendency will better prepare church leaders for their responsibilities and opportunities in the church unity movement at the local level.

D. CULTURAL ASSIMILATION. Still another social factor which operates in local church mergers is cultural assimilation, earlier noted in examining denominational mergers and the conciliar movement. The role of assimilation can best be depicted by considering a local church merger involving parties which stem from different ethnic backgrounds.

The LeSueur Presbyterian Church in LeSueur, Minnesota, offers such a case study. Its beginnings can be traced to the arrival of the Welsh, who settled the LeSueur prairie in southern Minnesota in the nineteenth century. These newcomers established and retained strong community ties and a clear-cut cultural identity in founding the Welsh-speaking Welsh Calvinist Methodist Church.

Although the original settlement spoke in the Welsh tongue exclusively, in time, the English-speaking public schools took their full toll. Employment of English in the church school coincided with its assimilation in the public school system. Beginning with a foreign language, the Welsh congregation became a bilingual and then an English-speaking parish.

Continuous contact with the wider community was maintained by the congregation. With the decline of the rural character of the community, the draining off of many young people to large cities and educational centers, and the gradual cooling of ardor for ethnic allegiance, the church was no longer able to support a full-time Welsh minister. It sought to share with the LeSueur Presbyterian Church a minister who spoke English solely. The Welsh congregation declined, while the Presbyterian Church grew with the growth of the town.

Finally on September 29, 1937, the merger between the two local parishes was consummated, having been facilitated by the organic union of their parent bodies. In addition, these social factors may be cited: the increasing use of the English language by the Welsh, the general decline of the rural-farming area and the consequent decline in membership of the Welsh Church, the use of the same pastor by both congregations, and intermarriage serving to cement closer relationships between members of both groups. With the assimilation of the Welsh both groups also shared in the prevailing common-core culture. Both groups were of similar socio-economic standing, since the Welsh represented a stable and financially independent farming group, while the Presbyterians were middle-class small businessmen. This instance of merger highlights the role of social factors and indicates that reduction in religious differences stems partially from reduction of social differences.

III. SUMMARY

This chapter has dealt with the various local community-centered churches—the independent, affiliated, denominational, and federated types. Some attention was given to reasons for the formation and development of each type. It was discovered that in each type social factors, and particularly social values, play a prominent role. Attitudes of laymen toward strictly denominational ventures have modified denominational loyalties, so that increasingly denominational churches serve the entire community. The erosion of such allegiances means that local churches typically have individuals of many denominational backgrounds in their membership. On the other hand, independent community churches have in many cases become affiliated with denominations. At any rate, the tremendous enthusiasm for independent churches, militantly antidenominational, is largely a thing of the past. Underscored in this chapter have been such social pressures as community social change; the impact of population mobility—both decline and growth—on urban, inner city, and suburban churches; the rise of suburbia; the values of efficiency, self-determination, and participation in voluntary associations; and cultural assimiliation.

7. The Comity Process

Last in our accounting, but no less important among unitive movements, is the comity process. A testimony to the ecumenical impact at the local level, the practice of comity has undergone rapid evolution. Its growth and changes during the last half-century have set in motion a process which has become deeply embedded in the patterns of the American church unity movement. Yet, because comity seems so commonplace in practice, and often matter-of-fact in detail, it largely gets overlooked in discussions of church unity.

This chapter seeks to examine the nature of comity, its structure and function (i.e., how it is organized and operated), some of its problems, basic principles, and social sources. Our discussion will focus on the local scene rather than on the national or denominational dimensions of comity.

I. THE NATURE OF COMITY

In a general sense, comity represents the co-operative effort of Protestants to meet the total religious needs of a given locality or community—so as to enable more effective ministries in terms of facilities, leadership, and program for evangelizing and nurturing people in the Christian faith. Comity is the process whereby churches develop joint planning and strategy in order to avoid "overlapping and overlooking." Given the diversity of Protestant groups in a community, the comity process acts as a

169

rational device for decision making and for the ordering of their mutual institutional concerns.

As one church leader bluntly stated the nature of comity, "It's comity or chaos!" Whereas earlier conceptions of comity stressed corrective and remedial action by avoiding duplication and neglect, today the emphasis is on positive and constructive measures which contribute to wise planning and church strategy. Earlier practices were based on "respect and good will." They dealt largely with settling disputes between churches with rival claims for church locations. These early relationships have been caricatured as interchurch "good manners"—"polite," "courageous," and "gentlemanly" relations. Today comity is viewed in more comprehensive terms: "a dynamic program of positive church co-operation to provide an efficient and inclusive pattern of religious service in every community." [1]

Newer conceptions of comity include: (1) Planning based on objective studies to determine the number and density of the population, prospects of population changes, physical and social trends of a community, religious affiliation or preference, and location and character of existing churches. (2) Systematic location and development of churches to provide each church with an adequate field of service, aid for established churches in meeting impending changes, safeguards for established churches when starting new ones, and adequate financial assistance during the formative period. (3) Highest possible standards of ministry and service to insure the type of program needed in the community, a ministry to all the people in the vicinity of the church, the location of new churches, and assurance that each church has a place in a broad fellowship of churches.

In recent years, the term "comity" itself has come in for considerable criticism and censure in view of its earlier connotations. Thus Ross W. Sanderson admonished:

Comity is another word made obsolete by the march of events.

[1] Statement of Department of Field Administration, National Council of Churches.

It is imperative that we cease to use it, that we find a better one. It is time we moved out of the kindergarten stage of well-mannered courtesy into the vigor of mature co-operative enterprises.[2]

There are many current efforts to abandon the term altogether in favor of an expression such as "co-operative planning and adjustment." Such attempts reflect the shift to a more positive notion of comity, and a desire to move beyond the more limited early conceptions and practices. Instead of dealing primarily with the adjudication of disputes, the recent focus emphasizes long-term planning and strategy for meeting the social changes confronting churches.

Two indicators point to the shift in recent years from a negative to a more comprehensive notion of comity. In the first place, new comity statements adopted by local councils have reflected the new outlook. A typical example appears in the statement adopted by the Council of Churches of Greater Cincinnati in 1948:

> The ideal toward which we strive is that comity shall not be the legalistic adjudication of controverted cases . . . but the blue-printing of a master plan within which all specific situations may be happily provided for. Specific proposals are not to be considered as cases brought by divergent and competitive interests, but rather as measures suggested toward carrying out our common purpose.[3]

Secondly, current names given to comity agencies reflect the changed outlook. Up to 1942, the term comity department or comity commission was used invariably. Today most of the local councils have changed these names, adopting such expressions as: "Church Planning and Strategy" (Washington State), "Survey, Planning, and Extension" (Southern California), "Church Planning and Adjustment" (New Jersey), "Inter-church Relations" (Pittsburgh), "Church Life and Develop-

---

[2] "A Challenge to Co-operation" (Address at the meeting of the Home Missions Council in New York City, January, 1946).

[3] H. Paul Douglass, *The Comity Report* (New York: Commission on Planning and Adjustment of Local Inter-Church Relations, 1950), p. 3.

ment" (New Hampshire), "Church Life and Extension" (Chicago and Cincinnati). Some councils, however, still preserve the name comity in their titles, for example, "Department of Church Extension and Comity" (Denver).

These new terms place the emphasis on co-operative planning and strategy, as the churches seek to confront community social changes. Moreover, they signify a rational, institutionalized procedure, which increasingly depends upon the specialized services of planning and research—a reliance upon sociological survey tools, rather than hit-or-miss, "by-guess-and-by-gosh" methods and personal agreements.

II. COMITY PRINCIPLES

One of the great values of the comity movement in the United States is that a set of principles and precedents have developed through co-operative experience. Not fixed or static, these principles are still in process of formation, particularly in light of changing comity conceptions. Yet it is possible to indicate some of the more commonly accepted principles, as follows:

1. Enough but not too many churches should be provided in each area.

2. These churches should be adequate in quality as well as in number.

3. Territorial fields can be allotted to competent denominations through comity procedures. Such allotment of occupancy should be protected for a reasonable time, until adequate churches are established.

4. In approving new enterprises or allotting fields the interests of existing groups should be safeguarded.

5. If control of the religious situation in a given community is assigned to co-operating denominations, every effort should be made to keep up with its changes and to maintain a just balance between the interests represented there.

6. Since a church allotted an area under comity represents all the co-operating churches, it should minister to all in the

community in an inclusive spirit, as a Protestant chaplain ministers to all denominations in the armed forces.

7. Denominational convictions must be respected, but adequate opportunity for all churches involves proper spacing and sufficient constituency. Reasonable place for service by minor denominations and groups should be provided in the total religious situation.[4]

These general principles are supplemented by more specific standards, which serve as guidelines for those bearing responsibility for comity decisions. A set of urban comity principles has been stated and revised by numerous interdenominational committees of the Home Missions Council and the Urban Church Department of the Federal and National Councils of Churches. Their full details are much too lengthy to be incorporated in this chapter. But some of the more salient features which indicate their import and the prevailing standards they convey may be presented:

1. An urban or suburban area shall be regarded as adequately churched when it has one church for each 1,500 to 2,500 available population of Protestant preference.[5]

a) Within a territory constituting a natural parish—i.e., one which is partly or fully enclosed by primary barriers, such as rivers, lakes, large parks, cemeteries, industrial installations, or multiple railroad tracks.

b) In which population is relatively homogeneous as to race and language, and

c) Exhibits social affinity for existing churches,

d) Is not connected with churches elsewhere; provided also,

e) That the existing churches receive into Christian fellowship all evangelical Christians.

---

[4] Department of the Urban Church, "Urban Comity Principles," *The City Church* (March, 1951).

[5] It should be noted that this is no dogmatic or fixed figure; some comity plans claim 2,000 to 4,000. For rural communities, the figure 500 to 1,000 is cited by the Town and Country Church Department of the National Council of Churches.

173

2. Determination of the size of the exclusive parish of a given church and the distance between churches should recognize that

a) Within a denomination churches should not be placed nearer than 1¾ miles:

b) And within Protestantism clustering may be permitted according to the density of the population of Protestant preference.

3. In urban situations, comity decisions must be made in the light of those prospective changes which are habitually characteristics of cities with the growth of peripheral and suburban areas.

4. Where there is declining population and deterioration in central and older urban areas the situation should be met by consolidation of existing churches, by the co-ordination of existing churches, by programs within a united church project, by orderly withdrawal or by the transfer of Protestant congregations of other races or tradition, or by adaptation of program.

5. There should be at least one strong Protestant church maintained in the downtown areas of every city.

These comity principles govern the urban church setting.[6] Several implications emerge from the elaboration of these principles. They have been forged through a process of interdenominational consultation and experience, representing years of planning and practice; they thus serve as definable norms of action; they seek to keep the churches alert to social changes in the community; they appeal to social factors—suggesting the military chaplaincy as a model, advocating racial and linguistic homogeneity as well as social affinity in the formation of churches. In addition, these comity principles are conducive to the establishment of community-centered churches in urging that a church serve its entire parish community.

---

[6] Supplementary principles are available for churches in small towns, villages, and rural areas. Cf. "Churching the Rural Community Co-operatively" (Commission on Comity Principles, National Convocation on Church in Town and Country, 1950).

III. STRUCTURE AND FUNCTION

The practice of comity is usually handled through a department or committee of the local council of churches. Comity comprises one of the major concerns of nearly every local council. Historically, it has been an integral part of the conciliar movement; generally, the stronger the local council, the more developed its comity department. In a few cases a comity commission operates independently or on a joint basis with the council of churches.

Ordinarily comity departments consist of official representatives of each co-operating denomination—local clergymen, laymen, and consultants. Official representatives likely include the denomination's resident executive or some formally designated person as his deputy. Laymen share in the committee's work in order to represent a cross section of church and community interest. Sometimes experts in city planning, research, or architecture are added as consultants. Officers of comity departments usually consist of a chairman—elected by the executive committee of the council of churches—a secretary, and various subcommittees appointed annually to deal with the many details which comity departments handle.

Comity operates on the local level through two somewhat different, though related, functions. The first function follows a fairly prescribed course of action for processing church extension requests, which come before the comity committee.[7] The second major function, which is newer, will be reviewed in some detail; it deals with long-term strategy and formulation of criteria for effective churches.

By assuming the function of planning and strategy, the comity department becomes the planning agency for the churches—a counterpart of the municipal planning commissions, which direct the future growth of a city in the best interest of all. As

[7] The routine steps for establishing new churches will not be detailed here; they may be found by consulting practically any constitution of an established comity department.

a planning agency, the responsibility of the comity department entails studying the social characteristics of the total community, tracing its social changes, and foreseeing what religious needs are unmet.

Comity also seeks to provide realistic and objective understanding of the typical problems facing churches in rural, urban, inner city, and fringe areas. Churches located in areas of rapidly expanding population or in neighborhoods of declining population particularly stand in need of common planning and strategy. All the more is this true for slum areas, industrial communities, and large housing developments—public or private.

With the recent development of planned communities, often built by a single developer, church sites must be selected at the blueprint stage, lest there be no available land or only improper locations (e.g., no provisions for offstreet parking facilities). Hence comity departments must negotiate with developers at an early stage. Frequently a comity department will purchase land and resell it after allocations are made to denominations. A positive conception of comity means that action in these new communities cannot be deferred until after the houses are all constructed and the people comfortably settled in them; for at the early building stage land is usually available and less expensive.

The important function of churching new communities in a patterned way through the practice of comity has become increasingly recognized, not only by denominations, but also by those agencies which must deal with churches. Thus one seasoned architect lends his support as he writes about formulating the master plan for the new Ford Development in Dearborn, Michigan:

Our job was made infinitely easier by the Comity Department, and if we might digress for a moment, the presence of this organization not only speeded the job, but will ultimately result in a more desirable church pattern. Such co-operative spirit should certainly be encouraged. This is a most important factor and one which reaches far beyond the church problem. With an honest atmosphere of Christian cooperation and sharing, we can surely proceed to greater and finer goals in city planning.[8]

Both private and municipal planners are generally desirous of consulting and working with church planners. But one can imagine the chaos of having to work separately with a variety of church planners. Protestant churches may take advantage of an important alliance with planners by acting as a unit through the comity department. As in the conciliar movement generally, Protestant co-operation is encouraged by having to deal with private and public agencies in unitive fashion.

Occasionally a comity department will recommend the establishment of interdenominational or community-centered churches, which are related directly to the comity department or to the council of churches instead of to a denomination. Already cited as an instance of this was the United Protestant Churches of Park Forest. The Constitution of the Department of Extension and Comity of the Denver Council of Churches states that interdenominational churches will be formed when the community involved definitely desires it and requests the Council's sponsorship, or when the community is not self-determining, as in the case of a public housing project or inmates of an institution. Similar provisions for sponsoring community-centered churches are provided in Southern California, Chicago, Cleveland, Cincinnati, and other councils of churches.

IV. PROBLEMS OF COMITY

Although the formal procedures and principles of comity are fairly well articulated, some critical problems remain. These negative features inhibit the process of comity from operating at its maximum or ideal level of efficiency. Such discrepancies are significant, for they reveal sources for the inducement of

---

[8] N. K. Van Osdal, Jr., "The Church and the Planned Community," *The City Church* (May, 1952), 9.

still further forms of changing practice in the ongoing development of the comity process. For church leaders, the identification of problem areas is important; for such knowledge bears on
the effective operation of the comity process, and serves as a
danger signal for church unity leaders to consider in their future
planning. We now seek to identify some of these difficulties:
*1. Unequal degree of power among denominations in a local
community.* To a large extent, the effective functioning of
comity depends upon its participants. Participation in a comity
department, as in so many other ecumenical agencies, is by
representation. Even when the religious groups are evenly represented in size, certain denominations in a particular community may wield a disproportionate amount of power. By
reason of its size or status or of the fact that it has within its
ranks the decision-makers of a community, a powerful denomination is often in a position to defy or evade comity procedures
and decisions. Or several denominations may combine against
a particular group, placing the weaker denomination in a dis-
advantageous position. H. Paul Douglass cites the case of one
denominational official who said to a council executive, "This
comity business is all right for the small fry, but when it comes
to moving our church, we've just got to have a location on the
Avenue!"
2. Unequal participation by member denominations. Some denominations do not participate wholeheartedly in the comity
process. Cases are recorded whereby groups proceed to renounce
and misunderstand policy decisions and understandings they
themselves helped formulate. Frequently a church goes ahead
on its own initiative and purchases a lot, and then appeals to
the comity department for approval. The department may ac-
quiesce in order to avert a crisis or to avoid embarrassing conflict, although it is convinced that the church is not entitled to
the location, or even that an additional church is not needed
in the community. A denomination may play only a limited part
in comity proceedings. Some denominations participate only in
a consultative relationship, largely for sharing information—

or to secure data it can ill-afford to miss—and for clearing of plans. Participation of some groups varies from community to community.

3. Inadequate social research as a basis for decision making. Frequently the more precise and painstaking task of survey and research is circumvented, and comity departments are satisfied with less than adequate social investigation, or none at all. As a substitute for social analysis to determine community needs in some comity situations, local pastors in the vicinity in question are asked whether they have any objections to the formation of a new church. If there be no major objections the allocation is promptly made. Such procedure is based on the older comity philosophy of good will, rather than on the newer concept of church planning. Another form of inadequate research for making decisions might be termed a "windshield survey." Such a survey consists of driving around the community in a car, making observations through the windshield, and then selecting a likely spot for a new church site. Comity committees frequently fail to utilize community resources—such as the city planning commission or the school system—where important and relevant community data await them. Even in instances where research personnel is available, frequently the studies employ questionable research methodology and report flimsy findings. Reconnaissance or nonintensive surveys generally represent the kind employed by comity departments as a basis for decision making. They are apt to be inadequate, because of their limited design and the rapidity with which they are executed. Yet the comity department is content to base its decisions on such inadequate social research.

4. Lack of systematic follow-through. Some comity committees assume that their responsibility ends when they earmark an allocation. Merely to designate an assignment is not sufficient. A denomination may fail to carry through its assumed responsibility; hence a breakdown occurs in the carefully planned strategy. Consequently a part of the community lacks adequate churching. The comity department must follow through on its allocation files to see that the denomination has fulfilled the terms of its assignment. Sometimes a denomination accepts a larger number of allocations than it can actually fulfill. Systematic follow-through entails reconsideration of cases from time to time and even reallocations, if commitments go unfulfilled. Planning and strategy phases of comity are particularly subject to neglect and inadequate systematic follow-through, as busy denominational executives and comity department members allow cases to remain dormant, or fail to keep abreast of community social changes.

5. *Non-co-operative groups.* If a large number of non-co-operative groups exist in a community the comity process may be stymied. Independent congregations, denominations which are not members of the council of churches, or various sect groups may refuse participation in the comity process, or may fail to recognize any of the decisions made. Such groups may wittingly or unwittingly take action which is contrary to comity recommendations. Thus resentment may ensue, or a "why-should-we-stick-by-the-rules-when-they-don't" attitude may be fostered. As a sort of retaliation the comity department or the local council will refuse to co-operate with non-co-operative groups. Such practice tends to drive a wedge between the co-operative and the non-co-operative groups. The spirit and ultimately the practice of comity are thereby strained.

6. *Failure to re-evaluate areas already churched.* Comity departments frequently fail to re-evaluate the religious situation in areas of the city not under discussion with respect to new churches. Normally, these will be some of the older and perhaps deteriorating sections of the city. For instance, there may be an inner city problem with the possibility of urban renewal or redevelopment. Perhaps a group of downtown churches are steadily losing ground, or a group of churches located in transitional areas may independently decide to relocate to the suburbs. Comity departments often fail to recognize their responsibility to see that the entire city is adequately churched; therefore, they tend to deal almost exclusively with the new,

expanding, "high potential" suburban developments. If comity seeks to fulfill its newer role of an enlarged concept of comprehensive community-church planning, then it must be concerned with developing strategies and assuming responsibilities for the churched as well as the unchurched neighborhoods.

V. COMITY AND ECUMENICITY

Comity reflects the ecumenical concern of Protestant churches. Such concern finds explicit expression in many constitutions of councils and comity departments. Thus the constitution of the Chicago Church Federation affirms that an "unbreakable unity" exists among the churches based on common loyalty to Christ and expressed in the co-operative activity of comity. In similar vein the Denver Council's Department of Church Extension and Comity asserts that the ultimate sanction for comity is the "conviction that all Christian churches are members one of another and should mutually share in planning." The Akron Council of Churches expresses a similar sentiment in its comity statement:

By mutual thought, planning and counsel, the churches co-operating in the Council of Churches will seek in accordance with the above principles to realize their united life within the Church Universal, as a body with many members locally responsible for adjusting their relations and organizing their work so as to perform the most effective Christian ministries to the entire community.[9]

Comity on the local levels points to an emerging system—co-operatively forged and rationally articulated—that has contributed considerably to local expressions of church unity in spirit and in fact. Significantly the practice of comity is performed in a co-operative fashion, calling for mutual consultation, and setting in motion processes for interchurch decision making. Interdenominational thinking and planning are at

[9] "Comity Principles for the Council of Churches of Akron" (Akron, Ohio: n.d.) .

work; a blow is struck against haphazard planning and against the detrimental kind of denominational rivalry and competitive acrimony characterizing interchurch relations of an earlier day. Since the deliberations and decisions of comity lack legal sanction, the only ultimate sanction for comity is the conviction that all Christian churches are "members one of another." In short, it is the ecumenical spirit which fosters comity practices and unites Protestant churches in common allegiance and commitment to the entire comity process.

The relationship between comity and ecumenicity is a two-way process. Historically this relationship is traced by Robert T. Handy, who documented the dynamic nature of comity in twentieth-century American Protestantism, concluding that "comity ever pushes on to some fuller form of unity" and prepares the way for other forms of ecumenical concern.[10]

Vivid examples of how comity reflects an ecumenical concern are discernible in cases of clustered churches—where several or more churches exist in close proximity. Often such churches compete and are more apt to form a clutter than a cluster. Under comity practices, it is not uncommon for such churches to strengthen one another by joint planning and action wherein each parish contributes its own uniqueness. In Philadelphia several denominational leaders met together to consider areas of the city where they were all trying to maintain work which was once flourishing, but now was struggling for survival. A common program was mapped out whereby various denominations assumed specific responsibility for given areas. It was agreed for some churches to be relocated; others were to remain and strengthen their program and outreach in service to the community.

A group of clustered churches often unite their forces to conduct more effective ministries. Under the aegis of comity the interdenominational fellowship is fostered and facilitated. The comity process has brought thousands of Christians together, calling them out of their isolation to focus on common

[10] *Op. cit.,* p. 172.

182

issues; it has been a vehicle for mediating potential strain and conflict. In the course of its work, it may share new insights and new appreciation for divergent viewpoints or unanticipated areas of consensus. Through such unintended consequences, making it possible to overcome denominational barriers and to bridge gaps in interchurch relations, comity may have an impact on ecumenicity far out of proportion to the relatively routine sphere in which it operates.

VI. SOCIAL SOURCES

At the outset of this chapter, our point of departure was the shifting focus of comity. Changing conceptions of comity bear some sociological significance. These changes give evidence of the institutional strain produced by less adequate, traditional forms of comity procedure. Changing institutional requirements of comity must be viewed in the light of heightened social changes in which new forms of comity need to be elaborated for an altered social context. Comity is a process enabling the maintenance of the institutional side of the church as an ongoing system in its particular tasks of redevelopment and extension. The mere structural existence of comity enables interaction of different religious groups. It is partly through such interaction that changes are mediated. In the epigrammatic words of Kingsley Davis, "Interaction is possible because there is a structure, and change is possible because there is interaction." [11]

Some of the social changes which induced new practices in the field of comity have already been noted in previous chapters. We need not repeat earlier points, except to select a few items and indicate their relevance.

Population migration and social changes in the ecology of our cities and rural areas, as discussed in the preceding chapter, have a profound impact upon Protestant churches. When families move from parishes in so-called stable and traditionally

[11] *Human Society* (New York: The Macmillan Company, 1948), p. 623.

established churches, some type of rational ecclesiastical planning and readjustment is mandatory. Conversely, population movement into new areas calls for co-operative planning to provide newcomers with adequate religious services. The challenge for co-operative planning through comity is dramatized by the knowledge that 31,000,000, or one out of five Americans annually change their places of residence.[12] Denominations seeking to co-operate in comity thereby profit from past mistakes of overchurching in confronting the institutional religious needs of mobile Americans.

In addition to population movements, increase in population at large and religious affiliation in particular has given added importance to the comity process as a means of meeting the need for new churches. Annual current rate of population increase is estimated as 3,000,000 by the Census Bureau. Present predictions are that the American population will climb to 225,000,000 by 1975. Obviously, increased population requires the building of new religious institutions to serve the growing population. Comity departments in many communities are already projecting plans into the future to meet the new needs. Even now it is estimated that some 6,600 communities in the nation stand in need of new Protestant churches.

Another drastic increase comes in building costs. Since 1940 construction costs have mounted more than fourfold. Many denominations have seriously depleted their building funds, while the need for new churches continues to be great. During the past decade Americans invested 4,000,000,000 dollars in

[12] This proportion has remained fairly constant over the past ten years, with young adults among the most mobile (41 per cent of persons 20-24 years old moved in 1957). Cf. U. S. Census Bureau, "News Release" (July 20, 1958). Other data showing the challenge for church extension follow: From 1940 to 1950 the St. Louis population increased from 816,048 to 852,523, but the suburbs jumped from 61,039 to 792,234. The Washington, D. C. suburbs grew six times as fast as the city itself. In Los Angeles, the city grew from 1,504,227 to 1,954,036, but the suburbs almost doubled, increasing over 950,000. Similarly, San Francisco's suburbs gained over 600,000 and New York's, about 700,000 between 1940 and 1950. Cf. Robert C. Cook, ed., *Population Bulletin* (Washington, D. C.: Population Reference Bureau, Inc., December, 1953), p. 89.

church building construction. Comity procedures function to meet the increased needs and the new evangelistic challenge with a minimum of waste and duplication and a maximum of wise planning and deployment of resources.

Population growth and redistribution present a challenge to church extension boards for the planning and financing of new churches. The bulk of these new church buildings are being erected in the so-called "high potential" or new residential suburban communities. This policy betrays an unavowed social source, namely, increased social class status achieved by the denomination at large with the addition of residential churches in these expanding suburban communities. Churches of this type are sometimes referred to by denominational officials as "affluent churches" and their members called "people of affluence." [13] Moreover, such churches in relatively short time become self-supporting, and can contribute financially to the work of the denomination. In short, from a business standpoint, they represent a good investment, since they are a potential source of substantial revenue.

Another factor giving rise to comity as an accepted, institutionalized instrumentality for carrying on co-operative relationships among the denominations is the increased mutual recognition of various religious bodies. Some denominations have established official policies for recognition and support of comity procedures. Other denominations, short of such policies, have issued statements commending comity as a legitimate means of working with other denominations. Such sanctions of national denominational groups tend to reinforce the practice and currency of comity at the local level.

Wherever population and ecological change call for institutional adaptation and new forms of church organization the comity process plays an important role. For comity aims to gear the churches to a state of readiness in confronting the incessantly changing conditions of the community. The growing

---

[13] The use of this phrase antedates the publication of the book by John K. Galbraith, *The Affluent Society* (Boston: Houghton Mifflin Company, 1958).

awareness and practice of comity has been called an expression of grass-roots ecumenicity. Its development is one sign of an acknowledgment by local churches of a common purpose and of the influence which the broader ecumenical movement has wrought in the lives of local parishes.

PART THREE

EVALUATION

8. The Countervailing Movements

On the basis of the evidence presented in the preceding chapters, ecumenical enthusiasts are prone to apply to the present period of interchurch relations such labels as "post denominational era," "time of ecumenical awakening," "the great reversal in Protestantism," "era of interchurch consciousness," and "age of the interdenominational mind." Before leaping to such sweeping conclusions, however, we must ask whether all the evidence has been scrutinized and, if possible, account for the countervailing movements.

The task of this chapter, then, is to test our interpretation of the rise of church unity movements in the light of organized expressions outside the drive for church unity.

Parallel to the rise of church unity—if not counter to it— has been the development of heightened forms of denominationalism, the rise of new sects, the resurgence of fundamentalism, and the rapid expansion of several large bodies such as the Southern Baptist Convention and the Lutheran Church, Missouri Synod. All these remain essentially outside the ecumenical fold.

At face value these various movements appear as countervailing factors. They seem to qualify, if not contradict, the thesis of the social sources of church unity. Further probing, however, indicates that the situation is by no means so simple and clear-cut. Although these movements may pose as parallel or counter trends, their relationship to ecumenicity is a dynamic one; in part they compete and in part they co-operate with the church unity thrust. In some cases, they relate to social factors in much the same way. New organizational unity among fundamentalists looms as a case in point. Instead of contradicting our thesis, these groups, which generally do not court church unity, may well confirm it.

The tendency toward church unity obviously does not imply uniformity of religious institutions. Doubtless new forms of diversity are developing. Social factors may still be conducive to schismatic ends, as evidenced in the failure of the Southern Presbyterian Church to ratify union with her two sister denominations to the North in 1955.[1] Yet the broad and dominant direction today is centripetal rather than centrifugal. Church unity is on the offensive! In the alternation between schism and unity, dominance has swung toward the latter pole.

Social factors may still play a divisive role, particularly evident in some cases of countervailing movements. Yet even the new diversities are susceptible to our main interpretation; for they represent new attempts at unity which, in no small measure, respond to the same social circumstances earlier detailed. In order to illumine these preliminary points, we will examine several apparently countervailing movements.

This chapter centers on the rise of denominationalism, the resurgence of sectarianism, the renewal of fundamentalism, and the remarkable Southern Baptist Convention. Our contention is that while these movements continue largely outside the drive for church unity—and to that extent remain divisive— in their very persistence they tend to illustrate and to lend greater confidence rather than to deny the thesis of the social sources of church unity.

I. DENOMINATIONALISM

Alongside the developing church unity movement, recent observers note significant signs of a ground swell in denomi-

---

[1] A careful study shows that while failure was attributed to doctrinal differences in the literature surrounding the merger, ecological analysis of the vote by presbyteries leads to the conclusion that the race issue is the major reason for failure. Cf. Sanford M. Dornbusch and Roger Irle, "The Failure of Presbyterian Union," *American Journal of Sociology*, Vol. LXIV, No. 4 (January 1959).

nationalism. An important distinction to draw between this newer development and the older situation is that denominationalism no longer implies schismatic defection, but rather the strengthening of older groups. Herbert W. Schneider commented:

> The growth of the ecumenical movement among Protestants . . . should not be interpreted as having undermined the diversified religious bodies of America. Though there have been a few mergers, the general denominational structure is stronger than ever.[2]

Perhaps Schneider underestimated the extent of denominational mergers and the intensity of the drive toward church unity. Mergers of institutions are imposing when weighed against the difficulty that as a rule institutions do not easily surrender their identity or transcend their self-perpetuating drives. Nevertheless, the contention that the general denominational structure is stronger than ever today remains difficult to refute. In many respects, the strengthening of denominations reflects the current American religious and cultural situation. Consider the contemporary revival of religious interest. Denominational structures exist as ready-made channels to receive and benefit from the so-called "return to religion" movement. Hence nearly every major religious group can cite ample statistics showing marked institutional growth in such areas as membership, church building fund campaigns, contributions to benevolences both at home and abroad, undergirding of church related colleges and seminaries, and the like.

On the other hand, an accentuated denominationalism cannot be attributed solely to the contemporary upswing in religion. One must also consider the special promotional efforts to extend the membership and further the program of the denomination. Truman Douglass cites a vivid instance of this endeavor:

[2] *Op. cit.*, p. 53.

The "denominational presupposition" . . . leads to the ecclesiastical equivalent of the dictum that what's good for General Motors is good for the country—that what is good for the denominations is automatically good for the Kingdom of God. And we have tremendous denominational sales organizations engaged in packaging this thought. . . .

I read the other day the words of an irrepressible huckster of one denomination's wares: "We believe that the next fifty years are going to be the glorious years of the ——————— Church. We believe that when we reach the year 2000, the United States will have a population of more than 275 million persons, and the ——————— Church will have more than 25 million members." [3]

The growth and intensification of the organizational machinery of denominations signify that these structures provide the necessary apparatus for fulfilling important functions which service the member churches. In a technological society where specialization is demanded and organizational life is complex, denominations which do not elaborate the organizational structures for co-ordination fail to cope with the functional requirements of large-scale institutional life. Thus the strengthening of denominationalism is largely a response to the cultural demands for specialized services and for the most efficient means of performing such services through centralized denominational agencies. Of course, the larger the denomination, the more elaborate and complex the organizational apparatus. More fully developed denominational machinery, therefore, is partly due to the increased size of the denominations in recent decades.

Confessionalism has been on the rise both in the United States and as a world-wide movement. Greater self-consciousness exists among such groups as the Alliance of the Reformed Churches Throughout the World Holding the Presbyterian Order, Lambeth Conference of World Anglicanism, Baptist World Alliance, International Congregational Council, Lutheran World Federation, World Convention of Churches of Christ, and the World Methodist Council. A number of these confessional bodies embrace groups which have common membership on the international level, but fail to have such fellowship on the national level. One such case is the leadership of the Southern Baptist Convention in the Baptist World Alliance.[4] These expressions of world confessionalism have been called ecumenical denominationalism or confessional ecumenism.

A widely held viewpoint among students of the ecumenical movement conceives of the resurgence of denominationalism as diametrically opposed to the rise of church unity.[5] Seen in this light, denominationalism is the antithesis of ecumenicity. Such a relationship between these two movements may be a facile, if not a false view. We have earlier advanced the notion that the two movements compete as well as co-operate with each other. Perhaps the evidence is insufficient to warrant the claim made by some that the denominations which make the best contribution to the ecumenical movement are precisely those farthest along in their self-consciousness. Nevertheless, some degree of truth obtains in this generalization. The relationship between denominationalism and ecumenicity is not solely antithetical. Let it be clear that this is not to speak in elliptical terms; for one can certainly cite instances in which denominational interests conflict with ecumenical ones. One must also acknowledge an interdependence between the two that scarcely seems recognized in ecumenical conversations.

Henry P. Van Dusen has called attention to the shaping of a new relationship.[6] The early leadership of the ecumenical movement came from outside rather than from within the ranks of official denominational leadership; today the leadership re-

---

[4] Of the twenty Baptist groups around the world which contribute to the financial support of the Baptist World Alliance, the Southern Baptist Convention provided $30,000 of the total budget of $58,028.50 for the year 1956.

[5] Cf. Charles C. Morrison, *The Unfinished Reformation* (New York: Harper & Brothers, 1953), pp. 26-73; and Arnold B. Rhodes, *The Church Faces Theisms* (Nashville: Abingdon Press, 1958), p. 175.

[6] "Councils in Crisis," *Theology Today*, IX (January, 1953), 501.

sponsibility has been transferred into the hands of denominational officers and official appointees. While difficult to relate causally, advance in ecumenicity and resurgence of denominationalism seem almost to go hand in hand. Financial support and participation in local councils of churches and in the National Council are largely channeled through denominations. Many local councils view themselves as instruments of the denominations. Comity is practiced by and through the denominations. Organic mergers and reunions involve denominations. Study groups, conferences, and conversations of an ecumenical nature are almost exclusively attended through representatives delegated officially by the denominations. In this sense, ecumenicity is dependent upon a denominational structure and can be said to support denominations.

Indeed, the church unity movement may not only strengthen denominations, but may also enable the denominational system to be more viable. As Robert T. Handy wrote in his history of co-operative home missions:

> The Councils did not seek to undercut the denominational system, but to strengthen it by avoiding duplication and conflict—comity—and by promoting joint planning—cooperation. The evil in ecclesiastical relations was traced not to the multiplicity of denominations, but to the lack of co-ordination among them.[7]

Advance in denominationalism and ecumenicity may go hand in hand, and they may not necessarily be rival movements. Support for this view comes from a council executive of a metropolitan area, who explained the basis on which the Council plans its program:

> The sole criterion by which our Council works can be measured by these two questions: (1) Is this program one in which there is a commonly recognized need by the denominations for co-ordinating their on-going efforts? (2) Is this activity one which the denominations recognize should be done, but which they cannot do themselves?

[7] *Op. cit.*, p. 35.

In light of the present-day pattern of religious institutions in America, effective forms of decision making and financial power reside in denominational structures. Should the major denominations decide to assert their autonomy, the organized forms of church unity (as discussed in this study) would suffer a serious set back—if, indeed, they could function at all. Hence we see that denominations not only compete but also function in co-operative ways in fostering and strengthening the church unity movement.

On the other hand, ecumenicity has modified the spirit, if not the form or structure, of the denominations. The readiness to merge forces and to co-operate at various levels of national and local religious life is a sign of a changed denominational posture. In some measure the denominations have appropriated and adapted into their own programs and policies the earlier thrust of the avowedly antidenominational community-church movement. Parish-oriented denominational churches ready to serve an entire community are today the rule rather than the exception. The number of intraconfessional mergers which have been consummated suggests that greater denominational self-consciousness may lead to organic unions within denominational families and not merely to isolation and exclusiveness.

In short, it is not altogether accurate to view the rise of denominationalism solely as a countervailing movement. Indeed, a good case may be made for the contention that the rise of denominationalism strengthens the development of the church unity movement, and that the strengthening of denominationalism responds to the institutional and cultural pressures of current American society.

II. SECTARIANISM

The resurgence of sectarianism is hailed as the "third great force" of historic Christianity.[8] Its swelling ranks claim the

---

[8] Henry P. Van Dusen, "The Third Force in Christendom," *Life*, 44 (June 9, 1958), 114.

renewed interest of churchmen of the "old-line" Protestant denominations. A few statistics will give some indication of sectarian extension: Assemblies of God increased from 6,703 in 1916 to 200,000 in 1939 and 505,552 in 1959. Likewise, the Church of the Nazarene grew from 6,657 in 1906 to 136,227 in 1936 and 291,036 in 1959. Doubtless the widespread growth of these newer religious movements shares partly in the general upsurge of religious interest in America.[9] Of course, the variety of sectarian expression is perplexingly complicated. Unlike the more "established sects," some sectarian groups call attention to themselves because of their high visibility and somewhat exotic, if not eccentric, qualities. As sectarian groups increase in size, they become centers of institutional power and potential threats to other religious groups.[10]

On the surface, it would seem that the rise of sectarianism constitutes a deviant case or a contradiction of our major thesis. Upon deeper analysis, however, the sectarian phenomenon actually provides a validation of our interpretation. The greater the degree of the sect's assimilation of its surrounding culture the less resistance it bears against the church unity movement.

[9] Statistics for sectarian growth as a whole may well be exaggerated. At any rate, reliable data would be desirable. For the established sects which reflect considerable growth, there may be countless other ephemeral groups which have declined or entirely disappeared from the scene. Enthusiasm for the growth of sectarianism must be tempered by this fact. A U.S. Census Report of Religious Bodies, like the last one in 1936, would shed considerable light on this problem.

[10] Perhaps no group expresses more alarm at the growth of sectarianism than the fundamentalists, who, curiously enough, themselves bear the taint of sectarianism. Books emanating from the fundamentalist presses about sectarianism are polemical, full of acrimony, and in many instances, are advertised as sensational exposés. Perhaps the latent reason is that fundamentalists are anxious to dissociate themselves from sectarianism as they themselves ascend in social status and respectability. This situation suggests a religious "henpecking" order of respectability!

Some of the polemical fundamentalist books are: Walter R. Martin, *The Rise of Cults* (Grand Rapids: Zondervan Publishing House, 1955) ; Walter R. Martin, *The Christian and the Cults* (Grand Rapids: Zondervan Publishing House, 1957) ; J. K. Van Baalen, *The Chaos of Cults* (Grand Rapids, Mich.: Wm. B. Eerdmans Publishing Company, 1956) , p. 14: "More and more I have come to the conclusion that we can learn from cultists, not only noting what not to believe, but also bearing in mind that the cults are the unpaid bills of the church!"

When social differences in class status, educational level, income, geographical isolation, and ethnic status are reduced, then
the sect is prepared to engage in ecumenical activities.

It is now a generally accepted view that sectarian groups
undergo radical change in the direction of accommodation to
the established churches and to the culture.[11] This development
becomes notably evident with the second and third generations,
when new members are "born" into the sect.[12] A process
takes place which Max Weber identified as "routinization of
charisma." General relaxation of the strict standards of the
founders sets in, particularly when the group expands, and
appeals are made for membership from the wider community.
A break-through comes in the previous isolation patterns,
which, in addition to doctrinal support, may be buttressed by
class, sectional, or ethnic differences or by distinctive styles of
life. As these barriers are reduced, sects develop more and more
into a denominational pattern, aping the more established
churches. In the meantime, as Reinhold Niebuhr suggested,
American churches adopt some of the sectarian tendencies. This
process makes for a gradual *rapprochement* between the two
groups. Hence Reinhold Niebuhr predicted. "It is safe to say
that the American churches (i.e., sects and denominations) will
achieve a broad working unity long before the vexing problem
of the Established and the Free Churches of Britain is solved.[13]

As the sectarian groups approximate similar cultural levels

[11] There is strong evidence indicating that accommodation is an adaptive response for the sake of survival, lest the group face organizational decline and
extinction. It is somewhat paradoxical that the alternative facing the sect is organizational extinction or the extinction of its original impulse or zeal. The choice
between upward social mobility and disintegration of the sect on the one hand,
or preservation of the sect at the expense of social mobility on the other, is discussed by Lloyd Warner, *Democracy in Jonesville, op. cit.*, p. 192.

[12] Of course, such sectarian groups as the Dukhoobors, Dunkards, Amish,
and Hutterian Brethren have persisted for generations relatively unchanged.
But they have generally done so through insulation from the surrounding
culture. There are even degrees of insulation within the same group, as a cursory
glance at the Mennonites would reveal.

[13] "The Ecumenical Issue in the United States," *Theology Today*, 3 (January,
1946), 534.

attained by the other denominations, their participation in church unity movements keeps apace. It may begin at the local levels with ministerial membership in local clergy fellowships, membership in councils of churches, and participation in the comity process. Affiliation is sought with various units of the National Council of Churches, perhaps as an observer at first, later as consultant and finally as a full member of the Council.

Our thesis that a reduction of social differences yields a re-duction of religious differences will be seen more clearly in a case study of the Church of God, Anderson, Indiana.[14] Its patterns of adaptation are fairly typical of other "established sects" such as the Church of the Nazarene, Seventh-Day Ad-ventist, Mission Covenant, Christian Missionary Alliance, and some of the Pentecostal groups.

In the Church of God one can trace the reduction of social differences, shifting from a sequence of conflict and withdrawal from society to accommodation, co-operation, and assimilation. In fact, a complete reversal of earlier patterns can be shown, as the group adapts to American culture, and especially to a common-core Protestantism.

Universally recognized and classified as a sect,[15] the Church of God originated in the 1880's amidst the largely rural setting of Ohio and Indiana. Its early founder, D. S. Warner, was nurtured in the holiness tradition. Growing out of discontent with the formality of organized Protestantism, the cooling of religious ardor, and the trend toward ecclesiastical centraliza-tion, the "Church of God Reformation Movement" sought to restore the authenticity of a Christianity marked by primitive New Testament simplicity. The early movement repudiated Protestantism as a corruption and a perversion of Christ's

---

[14] Data for this analysis are supplied through the courtesy of Val Clear, Pro-fessor of Sociology at Anderson College, and a member of the Church of God, Anderson, Indiana. Cf. Val Clear, "The Church of God: A Study in Social Adaptation" (unpublished Ph.D. dissertation, University of Chicago, 1954) ; and Val Clear, "The Urbanization of a Holiness Body," *The City Church*, IX (July-August, 1958) . Unless otherwise noted, citations are from the unpublished work.
[15] Clark, *op. cit.*, pp. 51 ff.

Church. It eschewed honorific titles, leveling all in its fellowship to biblical names, such as "brother," "sister," "saints," "elect." It adopted such rituals as foot washing, the "Holy Kiss," and "Holy Hands." It forbade its members to attend theaters, wear costume jewelry, or "fancy clothes." Indeed, its leaders did not permit the wearing of neckties. Later, when the movement began its accommodation, one of the internal controversies centered around the growing practice of wearing neckties.

Furthermore, explicit directions were given to its members to withdraw from participation in the political affairs of the outside world; members were even instructed to abstain from voting. The group shunned education and avoided formal education of its clergy, as long as they were "spirit led." Early leaders of the Church of God were extremely critical of the Federal Council of Churches. Other denominations also were scorned and ridiculed; they were called "apostate" and a "cancerous growth on the body of Christ." Emerging as the group did in protest against the growing organizational life and institutionalization of the church at large, it is hardly conceivable that co-operation with ecumenical bodies or with other churches would be viewed with favor.

Yet dramatic changes—imposed from external cultural pressures and internal desires to emulate "respectable" Protestantism—have so altered the contemporary pattern of the Church of God, that its early leaders would be unable to recognize it today as the "Reformation Movement" they founded. As Clear described it:

The process of adaptation has led the Church of God to build Church buildings of Gothic architecture, with divided chancel and other factors suited to sacramental churches rather than to the revivalistic "religion of the frontier" which has characterized the Church of God. Status and honorific religious titles have become current. "Reverend," "Doctor," and "Mr." gradually replaced . . . earlier designations. Originally regarded as a kiss of death, increas-

197

ingly pleasure is taken when a position of prestige is offered one of the group by an interdenominational body.[16]

Other dramatic changes have occurred in the style of life of the group. Coffee and tea, once linked with opium, are now commonplace drinks. Neckties, wedding rings, costume jewelry, and cosmetics are taken for granted. Novel reading and attendance at the theater is no longer frowned upon. Movies were once condemned, but when TV made its popular entry into the homes of Church of God members, movies came in through the front door. A fixed order of worship replaced the older "leading of the spirit" in worship services. Increasingly, the annual meeting is termed a convention instead of the traditional name, "camp meeting."

As for community participation and political activities, now Church of God members not only vote, but they frequently have an opportunity to vote for—or against—one of their own brethren running for public office. Members are urged to participate in politics, and not a few occupy influential posts. Like other Protestant clergymen, Church of God ministers belong to various community service clubs. Clear notes that "practically all the executives of the Church of God belong to Anderson's units of the Kiawanis, Lions, Optimist, or Rotary Clubs." [17] Instead of withdrawing from society, the Church of God has come to participate in virtually every phase of it.

Social factors were largely responsible for the virtually complete transformation of the sect. Detailed accounting would carry us far beyond our confines, but just to itemize: these included the process of institutionalization and centralization in response to organizational demands, the development of a college and seminary, outgrowing sectional confinement through geographical dispersion to every state in the union, shifting from a rural to an urban church, and ascendancy in socio-economic class status.

[16] *Op. cit.*, pp. 16 ff.
[17] *Ibid.*, p. 97.

As the Church of God adopted the values and institutional structures of "respectable" Protestantism, it also reached out in ecumenical relationships. Examples may be cited of new affiliations. Local congregations have joined councils of churches. The Board of Church Extension and Home Missions has co-operated extensively across denominational lines; it affiliated with the Home Missions Council, Interdenominational Bureau of Church Architecture, Interdenominational Spanish-Speaking Conference, Commission on Town and Country Church, and other like movements. The Church of God participates in the National Council's Division of Foreign Missions; it is a voting member of the National Council's Departments of Stewardship, of Evangelism, of United Church Women, and of the Commission on General Christian Education; in addition, it has consultant status in many departments and committees of the Council, of which it is presently an affiliate member. Clear noted a growing dissatisfaction with a less-than-full-membership status. It seems highly probable that eventually full membership in the National Council of Churches will be achieved. For "at every point of contact with the denominational world, the Church of God has tended increasingly to co-operate." [18]

The point to underscore in this discussion of the transformation of the Church of God from sect to church is that where social differences are reduced, the ground is prepared for the development of co-operative relationships, and ultimately for full participation in the church unity movement.

This finding receives corroboration from a similar study reported by Walter Muelder on the transition of the Church of the Nazarene.[19] Suffice it to present Muelder's conclusion at this point:

There are numerous hints even of co-operation and unity across previous barriers. With most of the major denominations the

[18] *Ibid.*, p. 372.
[19] "From Sect to Church," *Christendom*, 10 (Autumn, 1945), 450-62.

Church of the Nazarene has long been a member of the International Council of Religious Education. The First Church of the Nazarene . . . now co-operates with the Church Federation of Los Angeles. This trend is also apparent in some of the Assemblies of God, representatives of which are in the Women's Council. In Pasadena, the Nazarene churches co-operate with the Pastor's Union. . . . If the present trend continues, we may soon find the Nazarene Church quite fully participating in ecumenical organizations. This would mark a decisive step in accommodation to the church-type.[20]

On the national level, the Church of the Nazarene is currently a voting member of the National Council's Commission on General Christian Education and the Departments of Stewardship, of Evangelism, of Broadcasting and Films, and of the United Church Women.

We may conclude our analysis of sectarianism with the observation that contrary to superficial expectation, sectarianism —viewed in its dynamic relationship to the established common-core Protestantism and to American culture—does not necessarily contradict our thesis, but in many cases tends to validate it. For the erosion of social differences and assimilation to American culture and to a common-core Protestantism encourage participation in the movement for church unity.

III. FUNDAMENTALISM

Sizable groups of American Protestants remain outside the pale of the ecumenical movement. One such group might be loosely termed "fundamentalists," who take their cue from a particular interpretation of the authority and inspiration of Scripture. While fundamentalists are generally nonparticipants in the church unity movement, do they constitute a countervailing factor for our thesis? The evidence indicates the emergence of an independent, parallel movement for unity—a movement also responding to social sources. Before exploring its growing unity, let us first note the rebirth of fundamentalism.

[20] *Ibid.*, p. 462. Used by permission.

As a movement, fundamentalism enjoyed its greatest prominence in the last quarter of the nineteenth and the first quarter of the twentieth centuries. Although fundamentalist wings may be found in many of the major denominations, the movement as a whole declined markedly in influence after 1925. Now signs of a fundamentalist renascence reappear. One student of the problem observed:

There has been a remarkable renascence of intellectual activity among fundamentalist scholars. . . . The periodical *Christianity Today* has made its appearance, counting President Eisenhower's pastor among its contributing editors. The latest volume on apologetics from the pen of the president of Fuller Theological Seminary has been put before the public by a front-rank publisher.[21]

In addition to the renewed vigor on the intellectual front within fundamentalist circles [22] there is also the development of organizational unity running counter to the unity embodied in the National Council of Churches. A primary vehicle for expressing the new unity is the National Association of Evangelicals, organized in 1942 as a rallying-point for evangelicals.[23] The Association reports a membership of 2,000,000 in 1956, and a service constituency, through its commissions and affili-

[21] Arnold W. Hearn, "Fundamentalist Renascence," *Christian Century*, LXXV (April 30, 1958), 528-30.
[22] Some of the scholars who have published widely include Carl F. H. Henry, Edward J. Young, Edward John Carnell, John F. Walvoord, Bernard Ramm, J. Barton Payne, and Cornelius Van Til.
[23] Under the leadership of Carl McIntire, there is also the "American Council of Christian Churches" formed in 1941; it represents mainly two splinter groups —the Bible Presbyterians and the Bible Protestants. This organization of fundamentalists refuses to publish its membership statistics. The latest and most conservative of its many claims is 1,000,000 members, a figure which has been contested as a "deliberate distortion" by the National Association of Evangelicals. The American Council is avowedly an attempt to counter the ecumenical movement and has succeeded in creating considerable public confusion by its policy of holding its own meetings at the same time and near the same place as the larger ecumenical gatherings. For a detailed account of the questionable tactics and disruptive influence of the American Council of Christian Churches cf. Ralph L. Roy, *Apostles of Discord* (Boston: Beacon Press, 1953), pp. 185-250.

ated agencies, reaching 10,000,000 American Protestants.[24] Its membership includes forty denominations, many of them small religious bodies—such as General Six-Principle Baptists with 280 members, Grace Gospel Evangelistic Association with 1,000 members, and the Church by the Side of the Road with 2,000 members. The largest single group is the Assemblies of God with 400,000.

Generally critical of the ecumenical movement, some of the Association's spokesmen have directed stinging attacks against the Federal and National Councils of Churches. James De-Forest Murch, editor of the Association's bi-weekly organ, *United Evangelical Action,* referred to the National Council's formation as a "dangerous monopolistic move" and offered a long "bill of particulars" of the Council's inadequacies. The flavor of Murch's critique may be gleaned from the following excerpts:

1. The Council refused to adopt as a basis of fellowship the absolute minimum of fundamental evangelical Christian doctrine.

2. It admitted into its membership a host of "liberals" who were committed to a theology and philosophy which are definitely anti-Christian in the Biblical sense.

3. It created an organization which to all intents and purposes was under the rule of an "oligarchy." Real control lay in the hands of a few men who were definitely "liberal" in their viewpoint.

4. The ramifications of the Council were such that it was already beginning to function as a "Super-Church." [25]

Vigorous criticisms of the Federal and National Councils by some of the National Evangelical Association's top leaders are

[24] James DeForest Murch, *Cooperation Without Compromise* (Grand Rapids, Mich.: Wm. B. Eerdman's Publishing Company, 1956), p. 202.

[25] For other critiques of the Federal and National Councils of Churches, particularly on biblical grounds cf. J. Marcellus Kik, *Ecumenism and the Evangelical* (Philadelphia: Presbyterian and Reformed Publishing Company, 1958); and Chester E. Tulga, *The Case Against the Federal Council of Churches* (Chicago: Conservative Baptist Fellowship, n.d.), pp. 13, 21, 28, 33, 37.

directed as much at the Council's social and political liberalism as at its theological and biblical views. According to Ralph Roy:

Leaders of the National Association of Evangelicals generally tend to support ultra-conservative political, economic, and social views—although there are some exceptions. Their lack of the idealism that has characterized the mainstream of Protestantism has been typified in the Association's outlook on world affairs. Its Washington office, for example, has vigorously battled against UNESCO and the Universal Declaration of Human Rights.[26]

We have noted the resurgence of fundamentalism and its critical attitude toward the larger movement for church unity. Now it is apparent that fundamentalists have themselves coalesced and strengthened in organizational unity. The National Association of Evangelicals appointed its first executive director in 1948. It survived an internal financial crisis brought on by zealous overexpansion of program and activities in 1953-55, and has since become firmly rooted. In all probability, it will enjoy permanent institutional status on the American religious scene.

How should we account for the new organizational unity emerging among fundamentalists? These four points appear relevant: (1) Scriptural ecumenicity, (2) Counter-nucleation, (3) Social pressures, (4) Social concern.

1. Scriptural ecumenicity. The explicit and formal appeal to unity is based on a particular approach and interpretation of scripture. Regardless of inconsistencies in practice or deviations among the member groups, the manifest intention and charter proclaims what the president of the National Association of Evangelicals, H. H. Savage, calls "scriptural ecumenicity" as the basis and criterion of the organization's existence.[27] Such scriptural basis is not clearly defined, except to claim biblical sanction. Nevertheless, it provides the rallying cry for unity, around which the fellowship of the member groups is sustained.

[26] *Op. cit.,* p. 184.
[27] Murch, *op. cit.,* p. v. Also cf. Kik, *op. cit.*

Yet it forms only part of the picture; an adequate account of the new unity among fundamentalists must turn to social considerations.

2. "Counter-nucleation." The rise of unity within fundamentalism stems, in large measure, from the attempt to counter the power and institutional effectiveness in the unity movement developed by nonfundamentalists. Centralized organizational strength facilitates the ability to compete, lest the movement suffer in influence. This contention receives vigorous backing in Murch's history of the National Association of Evangelicals; he points out case after case in which fundamentalists had "lost out to the liberals and modernists." Some instances are the desire for a national evangelical publication and press, lest the field be pre-empted by the adversaries; the struggle against comity, which "denied rights to Bible-believing churches," thereby making it necessary for the Association to "present evangelical claims to the American Institute of Planners and to other nonreligious authoritative bodies"; [28] the opening of a Washington, D. C., office with particular responsibility for representing fundamentalist groups in the appointment of chaplains for the armed services; the most dramatic struggle, which has been largely successful for the Association, is what Murch calls "the rescue of evangelical broadcasting." When it appeared that the Federal Council of Churches had a virtual monopoly of sustained religious broadcasting time, the Association's concerted pressure actually resulted in a change of policy by many of the major networks; these networks now offer a proportionate share of "sustaining time" to broadcasters approved by the National Association of Evangelicals.

As a matter of fact, the Association's developing organizational unity and increasingly nation-wide scope makes it look like a faint carbon copy of the National Council of Churches, against which it has so frequently inveighed.[29] In an organizational

[28] *Ibid.*, p. 118.

[29] A leader of the Inter-Varsity Christian Fellowship, a conservative student group, expressed his concern that the building of the Inter-Church Center on

sense there is parallel duplication of offices, boards, and agencies. Like the National Council, the National Association has an executive staff, regional offices, and some local associations; a Washington, D. C., office; chaplaincy commission; radio-TV commission; higher-education, Sunday-school, and youth commissions; foreign-missions division; national fellowships for laymen and laywomen; social-action commissions; world-relief commission; publications department and a national journal; and a number of functional commissions, such as evangelism and stewardship. Finally, it is related to a world body, the World Evangelical Fellowship, having played an instrumental role in instigating this world organization.

3. *Social pressures.* Unity in fundamentalist circles is partly a response to similar social pressures which encouraged the formation of the National Council of Churches. At first glance the interpretation of developing unity among fundamentalists in response to external social stimuli may seem like a platitudinous point which hardly needs laboring. Yet recall that traditionally fundamentalism has sought to resist social change. Indeed it often takes a certain pride in the ability to stand fast and employs the term "compromise" as an epithet for theological liberalism. John Dillenberger and Claude Welch suggested that resistance to social change goes along with a fundamentalist mentality to preserve certainty in a world of apparent confusion,[30] and Stewart G. Cole, in his *History of Fundamentalism,* maintained:

The fundamentalist was opposed to *social change*—particularly such changes as threatened the standards of his faith and his status in ecclesiastical circles. Those churchmen who attempted the task

Morningside Heights, next to Union Seminary and Riverside Church, is evidence of the development of a "Vatican of American Protestantism." He suggested renaming Morningside Heights, "Vatican Hill." Also cf. G. M. Savery, "Do We Want a Giant Church?" *Christianity Today* (April 29, 1957), 8-9.

[30] Cf. *Protestant Christianity Interpreted Through its Development* (New York: Charles Scribner's Sons, 1954), p. 231.

of re-defining Christianity to meet the conditions of shifting culture became known as "modernists." [31]

In order to arrest their dwindling influence, fundamentalists have felt the need for a co-operating agency, a centralized, co-ordinating body to perform important functions and to exercise effective influence on the American scene. The social context and cultural pressures demand such an organizational structure for corporate expression and action, lest strength be dissipated in the face of emerging unity among non-fundamentalists. Viable relationships with the federal government, with national agencies, and with the centers of mass communication cannot be established in any effective manner by forty separate groups of fundamentalist persuasion. As the editor of the Association's official magazine observed:

> Prior to the beginnings of the Association in 1941-42, these advocates of the historic evangelical Christian faith were divided and impotent. . . . They were an "unvoiced multitude" yearning for some adequate medium through which they might present their evangelical testimony to the nation and work together for the accomplishment of common purpose.[32]

4. Social concern. A fourth factor, related to the previous one, is the unity arising out of social concern. Let us acknowledge that the evidence for this fourth factor is less substantial than in the previous instances. Our discussion of fundamentalism's resurgence began by noting new signs of intellectual ferment in fundamentalist circles. A considerable group of fundamentalists have earned doctorates from such academic institutions as Harvard, Boston, Chicago, Basel, and Zurich. It would not be amiss to suggest that these individuals increasingly play an important role in the present-day fundamentalist movement. One possible sign of their influence comes

[31] *The History of Fundamentalism* (New York: Richard R. Smith, Inc., 1931), p. 53.
[32] Murch, *op. cit.*, p. vii.

precisely at the point of growing concern for social justice as a basis for unity within fundamentalist ranks.[33] In a searching book, which appraises the lack of concern for social issues, an articulate spokesman of fundamentalism, Carl F. H. Henry, called for unity to face social needs. With such forthright expressions as "embarrassing divorce," and "uneasy conscience," Henry called upon fundamentalists to confront pressing social issues in unitive response:

Evangelical convictions need a united voice. . . . If, as is often remarked, the Federal Council of Churches is the voice of Protestant liberalism in America, Protestant evangelicalism too needs a single voice. When such a unity comes, the present competitive spirit of evangelical groups shall be overruled to the glory of God.[34]

Our analysis of organizational unity among fundamentalists as a parallel to the church unity movement, in response to similar social stimuli, should not imply rigidity in the relationship between the two movements. Assimilation of some fundamentalist individuals and groups has taken place, particularly at the local level of the conciliar movement and in some federated community churches.[35] That any large-scale assimilation will occur is highly improbable. More likely, the large group and the smaller one will function along parallel lines, with a considerable amount of competition and some small degree of co-operation, especially on local levels. In all likelihood, the National Association of Evangelicals will continue to grow in

[33] Hearn, op. cit., p. 528.
It was reported to me that the official correspondent for Christianity Today, at the Oberlin Conference on Faith and Order sponsored by the World and National Councils of Churches, found it extremely difficult to disagree with the Conference proceedings and findings as he was preparing his report of Oberlin.
[34] The Uneasy Conscience of Modern Fundamentalism (Grand Rapids: Wm. B. Eerdmans Publishing Company, 1947), p. 81.
[35] "As Edwin M. Poteat observed, whereas once the common folk had been taught by their ministers to consider Fosdick the supreme heretic, with the radio they could hear the man and discover that his doctrines were not, after all, the instruments of Satan." Quoted by Norman F. Furniss, The Fundamentalist Controversy, 1918-1931 (New Haven: Yale University Press, 1954), p. 180.

organizational strength and in service to its constituency. With more intensive institutional growth, the character of the Association may be altered in unanticipated ways; in the process it may conform more and more to the larger church unity movement, at which it presently hurls invectives.

If the resurgence of fundamentalism can be considered a parallel movement for unity, perhaps it is salutary to suggest the relevance of our interpretation of social sources in relation to the growing organizational unity found today among fundamentalists. It may well be that in addition to "confessional ecumenism," some such term as "fundamentalist ecumenism" needs to be coined to refer to this phenomenon.

IV. SOUTHERN BAPTIST CONVENTION

On the surface it appears that a very definite countervailing factor is posed in the case of the Southern Baptist Convention. One of the nation's most rapidly growing religious groups, its membership was 9,202,205 in 1959, a gain of 245,449 members over 1958. Second in size only to The Methodist Church, the Southern Baptist Convention is conspicuous by its absence in the ecumenical movement. Dubbed by some critics as the "problem child of American Protestantism," it has rejected invitations to join the Federal, National, and World Councils of Churches.

It seems to defy any easy generalization or framework of interpretation. At one time it could be fairly certain that the Southern Baptist Convention was a regional phenomenon, but it has spread like a prairie fire to the Northeast, Mid-West, and West Coast. It is represented in Alaska and seems to respect only the boundaries of Canada.[36] In several Northern states, such as Illinois and Indiana, Southern Baptist churches outnumber those founded by the American (Northern) Baptist Convention.

As a rule Southern Baptists stay ouside the ecumenical move-

---

[36] According to a *New York Times* report, the 1958 meeting of the Southern Baptist Convention voted to honor the request of Canadian Baptists to refrain from evangelizing over the border.

ment. Recalling our thesis—the reduction of religious differences stems partially from the reduction of social differences
—we shall examine the extent to which the Southern Baptist
case indicates that since social differences persist, religious
separation remains. To the degree that social differences are
maintained, our thesis of the social sources of ecumenicity still
stands.

Three factors may be singled out for analysis: (1) sectionalism, (2) institutional success and power, and (3) race.[37]
Let us stress again however, that no simple explanation can
cover all the complexities and variabilities embodied in this
denomination.

1. Sectionalism. Despite their rapid spread to other regions,
the Southern Baptists remain dominantly a Southern group
in many respects, deeply enmeshed in the *mores* and traditions
of a way of life which is shaken, but not terminated. We have
earlier noted rapid social changes tending to alter sectional
patterns, notably in the South. Also previously discussed was
the underdeveloped status of councils of churches in Southern
cities. The process of sectional erosion is by no means evenly
distributed among the various institutions of society. One cannot overlook the strength of sectionalism as a "survival" factor
in the Southern Baptist situation. In such states as Mississippi,
Georgia, and Alabama the concentration of Southern Baptists
is so great that it has been likened to a "state church." Let us
not forget that these are three states where school desegregation
has made literally no progress. The combined strength of delegates and ministers from these three states at a convention can
almost veto any proposal before the house. In other Southern
states too—Texas, South Carolina, Oklahoma—the Southern
Baptists are the overwhelmingly dominant group. Such sectional concentration leads to the rise of institutional insulation.

[37] These three factors are not necessarily equally weighted. For example, the
racial factor probably plays a less decisive, though not negligible, role. It must
nevertheless be considered as an important aspect of the cultural milieu in which,
for the most part, the Southern Baptist denomination exists.

Various groups represented in the South (e.g., Methodist, Southern Presbyterian, and Disciples) have ties with national bodies or belong to the National or World Council of Churches; these national groups have their strength distributed in other parts of the nation. Such ties tend to mitigate group insulation and function to reduce social differences. The Southern Baptist Convention has relatively little formal relationship with outside groups.[38] Its dominant seat of power resides in the Deep South, tending thereby to reinforce its insulation. This view is confirmed in an official publication of the Home Mission Board: "By some strange providence, Southern Baptists have been fenced in by political and economic conditions. . . . They have been isolated, socially, politically, economically, and religiously." [39]

To the extent that social differences have not been appreciably reduced or transformed in their actual function, the Southern Baptist Convention's lack of involvement in church unity is consistent with our thesis of the social sources of ecumenicity: where social differences have been reduced, the movement toward church unity is enhanced; contrariwise, where social differences remain, the drive for church unity is not favored.

2. Institutional success and power. Partly related to sectional concentration is the fact that the group's very strength gives it a high degree of self-sufficiency and independence. Institutional success, as the "fastest growing" church in America has contributed to denominational aloofness. A pronounced program of evangelism adds membership strength. To state the matter bluntly, the Southern Baptist Convention stands to gain nothing —in an institutional sense—from co-operation with other Protestant groups. Where it outnumbers all the other denominations combined, as in a few states, and where in every Southern state

[38] For example, one is not aware of Southern Baptists' involvement in merger proposals or negotiations to unite the twenty-seven Baptist groups now in existence, or to discuss merger with other denominations. Such is not the case with the Disciples or the Southern Presbyterians.

[39] J. B. Lawrence, *Cooperating Southern Baptists* (Atlanta: Home Mission Board, Southern Baptist Convention, 1949), pp. 7 ff.

it is the majority group—with the single exception of Louisiana where Roman Catholics are slightly larger—then the urgency to co-operate with other bodies is seriously curtailed. The functional need for co-ordination of competing and potentially conflicting denominational groups is minimized. In some cases, the more pressing problem seems to be mutual rapport with brethren of the same group.

Their power and sectional dominance, remarkable growth as a result of an aggressive program of evangelism,[40] and comparatively sectional isolation have afforded Southern Baptists a degree of autonomy. These factors have largely given rise to the attitude of separation from the mainstream of the church unity movement. It is important to acknowledge the institutional success and vitality of the Southern Baptists. To taunt the movement with such labels as "problem child" probably only intensifies its sense of solidarity and self-sufficiency.

3. Race. A third social factor which functions subtly is the race issue. In an earlier chapter we noted rapid social changes as well as patterns of resistance, most dramatically evident in some Southern states. Despite the fact that the Convention has officially passed resolutions endorsing the Supreme Court's ruling on desegregation in public schools, the gap between profession and practice is prominent; for the bulk of rank-and-file members, particularly in the Deep South, are hostile to the Court's decision. Many Southern Baptists would protest against the National Council's policy of a "non-segregated church in a non-segregated society." Even when they support the National Council's stand through resolutions, other charges against the Council—such as associating it with socialism, planned economy, attention to social issues rather than regeneration, and violating the coveted doctrine of separation of church and

---

[40] Between 1929 and 1952, Southern Baptist membership increased 102 per cent —more than twice the increase of the Roman Catholic Church for the same period. One often hears the facetious remark that if Southern Baptists continue to grow at their present rate, there will be more Southern Baptists than people at the turn of the century.

state—these charges tend to nullify the principle.[41]

Needless to add, where racial fears function as a covert issue, many Southern Baptists are merely mirroring the prevailing cultural values of their community. The unresolved race problem, then, plays some role, directly or covertly, in the decision of Southern Baptists to remain largely outside the church unity movement.

Having considered the three social factors as among the reasons for inhibiting ecumenical participation, we must now turn to the official reason given for rejecting the World Council's invitation—namely, the lack of authority; it is stated in the Convention's minutes as follows:

> The Southern Baptist Convention is a voluntary association of Baptists for the purpose of eliciting, combining, and directing the energies of our denomination in missionary activity at home and abroad, and in educational and benevolent work throughout the world. Our Convention has no ecclesiastical authority. It is in no sense the Southern Baptist Church. The thousands of churches to which our Convention looks for support of its missionary, benevolent, and educational program, cherish their independence and would disapprove of any attempted exercise of ecclesiastical authority over them.
>
> In a world which more and more seeks centralization of power in industry, in civil government, and in religion, we are sensible of the dangers of totalitarian trends which threaten the autonomy of all free churches. We wish to do nothing that will imperil the growing spirit of co-operation on the part of our churches in the work of giving the Gospel of Christ, as we understand it, to all men everywhere. In the light of these considerations, we feel impelled to decline the invitation to membership in the World Council of Churches.[42]

Despite the reason given for declining the invitation, observers have noted that the Southern Baptist Convention does

[41] Cf. William R. Estep, *Church Union and Southern Baptists* (Fort Worth: Baptist Book Store, 1955).

[42] *Annual, Southern Baptist Convention* (1940), p. 99.

appear to have *de facto* authority to legislate for its member churches. Indeed, it does so at every meeting of the Convention. It establishes quotas and requirements of membership and financial support; it sets goals for denominational extension. Notwithstanding carefully worded disclaimers based on a rather unique interpretation of congregational polity, the Convention and its professional staff (operating through boards) are functionally the equivalent of other denominational headquarters and staff, despite the different terminology employed. As we discovered in our earlier discussion of organizational structure, the authority and institutional power a Southern Baptist executive wields is equal to—if not greater than—that found in other forms of polity.

On the specific issue of the Convention's authority, one Southern Baptist leader, Theron D. Price, contended:

> With specific reference to our participation in the World Council of Churches: It is obvious that there is nothing distinctively Baptistic to prevent it. Numerous other Baptist Conventions or Unions are able to co-operate on terms which threaten neither our doctrine nor our polity. We could, on principle, co-operate—in such way as to jeopardize none of our principles, and without construing our Convention as a Church. But for various reasons and convictions, as well as prejudices and fears, we have refrained, and probably will continue to refrain from participation.[43]

While individual Southern Baptists may vary considerably in their attitudes toward the church unity movement, taken as a whole, the stance of the group is highly critical. In fact, extreme expressions of disfavor and denunciation are sometimes charged by the group's leaders. Criticisms of the Federal, National, and World Councils include such disparaging charges as "coercive," "giant organization," "separatist," "totalitarian," and "antidemocratic." J. B. Lawrence, former executive of the Home Mission Board, wrote:

[43] "A Southern Baptist Views Church Unity," *Church Unity in North America*, ed. J. Robert Nelson (St. Louis: Bethany Press, 1958), p. 88.

Some ministers and laymen are so charmed by the siren-voiced promoters of this totalitarian Protestant idea, that they do not see the ungloved hand of regimentation lurking in the shadows of sweet-voiced sentences, ready to grasp churches, pastors, and people with its totalitarian authority.[44]

The final word in considering the Southern Baptist Convention as a possible countervailing factor must express something of the internal dynamics taking place within the group. As the pastor of Atlanta's influential First Baptist Church pointed out: "It must be recalled that in three decades the Southern Baptists have changed from a primitive fundamentalism to a social consciousness and a gospel of relevancy."

A small, but increasingly restless and vocal, minority of Southern Baptist ministers adhere to liberal racial and political policies and are in full accord with the ecumenical movement. Although this group by no means sits in the high places of power and control, its representatives may be found occupying some important teaching posts and pulpits. Generally, but not exclusively, this significant minority is found among the younger ministers who received their seminary training at such institutions as Louisville, Southeastern, Colgate-Rochester, Andover-Newton, Crozer, Yale, and Union.[45] One cannot lightly discount the long-term impact of these younger ministers—who stay within the fellowship, since many are tempted to leave it— on the denomination as a whole and on its attitudes toward ecumenicity. While the eventual outcome cannot be foreseen, two "signs" merit recording.

The first is that Southern Baptists already co-operate in a few interdenominational ventures, such as the National Council's Department of Stewardship, Church World Service, United Church Women, and various committees of the Commission on General Christian Education—formerly the International Council of Religious Education. Precisely what relationship

[44] *Op. cit.*, p. 86.
[45] Some Southern Baptist seminaries, following the early lead of Louisville, have a fine record of interracial student body enrollment.

Southern Baptists have to the Commission on General Christian Education is somewhat baffling even to professional ecclesiastics. Southern Baptists hold full membership on the Uniform Lesson Committee—a sub-committee of the Commission—but are not members of the parent Commission. On the Committee on Religion and Public Education, the Southern Baptist representative is listed as a member-at-large. Notwithstanding official labels adopted, informed sources report that Southern Baptist members of these committees behave and function as full-fledged members. In addition, during the early stages of the ecumenical movement—from 1911 to 1927—Southern Baptists were active in the Faith and Order Movement.[46] At the Oberlin Conference, two delegates participated actively, although officially they were listed as observers. On the local level, one Southern Baptist leader gravely advanced the exaggerated claim that Southern Baptists enjoy the "finest sort of fellowship between the churches; in practically every city there is a Protestant minister's conference or council (of churches) in which all the ministers have or can have membership."[47]

Our final point concerns the transformations taking place in the South, particularly industrialization, urbanization, and the erosion of sectionalism earlier reviewed. As the cultural status of various regions in America become more nearly alike, modification in other institutional spheres will result. Exposure to the common influence of national life will undoubtedly continue at an accelerated pace in the decades ahead. The spread of the denomination to other sections throughout the nation may eventually contribute to undermine its sectional isolation. A case in point is the establishment of the Golden Gate Baptist Theological Seminary in Berkeley, California—a large training center for Southern Baptist seminarians, many of whom are recruited from the South. Many Southern Baptist ministers and laymen, who at the moment may be enjoying

[46] Cf. *Annual, Southern Baptist Convention,* 1913-16.
[47] Lawrence, *op. cit.,* p. 97.

a newly found middle-class status, may well witness an inevitable atrophying of their sectarian tendencies.

It would be too optimistic to conclude that a combination of these and other social forces will eventually break down the resistance of Southern Baptists to church unity. Nevertheless, one must properly view the Southern Baptists and the church unity movement as both in process and development. Hence the future relationship between the two is unpredictable. We might well conclude our analysis with this observation: the Southern Baptist Convention today plays an ambiguous role. It represents a countervailing factor to the extent that its non-participation in church unity is not exhausted by interpretations rooted in social factors. But to the degree that such factors as sectionalism, institutional power, and race obtain, the Southern Baptist Convention affirms—albeit negatively—our thesis of the social sources of church unity.

9. Concluding Postscript

As the study draws to its conclusion, we are left, as it were, with needle and thread in hand, wondering what kind of consistent and coherent pattern has been woven. Recall that the common thread of interpretation weaving its way through this book is that social unity—broadly conceived—is conducive to church unity. Recall too that in dealing with its social sources, we have not sought to give a "blanket" interpretation.

We must confess that church unity is, indeed, a many-factored thing. An interpretation of the social dimensions of the church unity movement, if presented as a sufficient viewpoint, would be grossly inadequate. Instead, it has been our intention to offer a framework of interpretation from a particular standpoint, which would illumine the contemporary surge in the movement toward church unity. It is by no means the only interpretation of this complex phenomenon. On the other hand, it is an important one, and one which is frequently neglected or obscured, or worst, misrepresented, when social considerations are judged solely in pejorative terms.

After detailing the signs of cultural unity in Part I, various expressions and institutions of church unity and their relationships to social factors were examined in Part II of this study. Although we noted earlier stirrings, the full force and flowering of ecumenicity have not been a decisive factor in American Protestantism until the present century. In recent decades, its accelerated pace is evidenced by the different mood governing the interrelations among Protestant groups, and by the emergence of rational organizational structures as vehicles for ecumenical concern. These processes and institutions of church unity operate at various levels and exert a profound influence on religious life in America.

Nationally, they may be found in the denominational mergers and reunions, in the development of the Federal and National Councils of Churches. Local forms include councils of churches, community-centered churches, and the comity process. In addition, there is the emergence of a common-core Protestantism, a common tone and a unified pattern shared by the bulk of Protestants, suggesting a functional convergence and an erosion of the allegiance to denominations.

Operating either covertly or explicitly in these movements for church unity are social and cultural pressures. Cultural values, such as efficiency, co-operation, self-determination, and participation have supplied strong ideological supports. The reduction of social differences and increased affinity to a common-core American culture have overcome resistance and eroded earlier barriers to church unity. In some cases, the erosion of the topsoil of cultural diversity has exposed common roots which serve to facilitate religious unity. Recent developments in American culture, such as population mobility, the mushrooming of suburbia, the trend toward organizational centralization, the rapidity of social change, and the rise of urbanization are among the social sources contributing to the drive toward church unity.

Appropriate summaries of the main argument are advanced at the end of each chapter. Hence there is little need for repetition of these many points, save as our thesis requires succinct restatement and brief indication of its relevance.

1. The surge of the church unity movement in the United States has been favored by social and cultural forces. Social conditions, as H. Richard Niebuhr convincingly documented in his *Social Sources of Denominationalism,* spawned divisiveness in church and society. Such an interpretation, however, cannot be saddled to social conditions which no longer obtain.

These social sources have been largely mitigated, and in the contemporary scene are less likely to provide the occasion for church disunity. Instead, a growing cultural unity and cohesiveness in American life has reduced social differences and disrupted patterns of insulation, which formerly separated the Protestant religious bodies.

2. The growing sense of unity and the reduction of social cleavages (e.g., class, sectionalism, nationality, and race) have altered the older social foundation for religious proliferation. As social differences recede into the background, common allegiances are coming to the fore. Hence the emerging cultural unity provides a new base for the reflection of church unity. The minimizing—though not the disappearance—of the older bases of social differentiation and the rise in the movement toward church unity—this is the nexus explored in our study.

3. The stream of church unity in American Protestantism flows along many channels. We have sought to demonstrate in detail the social sources of each of the various forms of church unity, noting that the emergence of a common-core Protestantism reflects the common-core culture of American society. As diverse religious groups of racial or sectarian, ethnic or sectional character come to share or emulate the common-core Protestantism, they participate more fully in the church unity movement. Common-core Protestantism provides much of the subsoil for the fertile growth of ecumenicity.

4. Organic mergers within denominational families and across denominational lines are facilitated by the reduction of social disparities between the uniting bodies, as differences—stemming from ethnic backgrounds or sectional interests represented by the uniting groups—are overcome, or as successive waves of the same immigrant group, are assimilated to a common-core American culture. This process is particularly evident in the decline of the foreign language in favor of the use of English. Denominational organic mergers further reflect a cultural trend toward organizational "nucleation" and the de-

219

sire for institutional strength to counter and relate to other centers of religious and secular power in the nation.

5. The conciliar movement is a rational organizational structure to perform necessary tasks and to fulfill the need for functional co-ordination, growing out of the increasing interdependence and heightened organizational life of American society. On the national level, it is oriented to the national ethos, policies, and private and public agencies of nation-wide scope, whereas local councils of churches are oriented to community counterparts. In large measure, the local conciliar movement depends upon the size of the city—the larger the city, the more complex the council's organizational structure. Every city over 200,000 in population contains a council of churches. Every non-Southern urban area of 100,000 or more claims a council. The conciliar movement is a vehicle for integrating the multiplicity of religious groups and for the expression of corporate action in prescribed areas.

6. Local community-centered churches, of which there are four basic types, are increasingly a product of the self-determination of prospective members, reflecting their cultural values of independence, belongingness, and efficiency. The development of community-centered churches closely relates to social changes in the community—particularly sudden population shifts in or out of the neighborhood. In many declining communities and small rural areas, the formation of community-centered churches is an adaptation for the sake of institutional survival. In new suburban communities, the high degree of neighboring and common social backgrounds, interests, age level, occupation, styles of life, and income are conducive to social cohesiveness, which is in turn reflected in the organization and life of the community-centered suburban church.

7. The practice of comity is an institutional device for joint planning and co-operation among denominational leaders. Through the comity process social changes in the community may be anticipated and dealt with, and competition and over-churching can be minimized. Comity constitutes a necessary

and rational structure for administration and for economic and orderly development of new churches, in view of the proliferation of new communities and increased population mobility and population growth of American society.

8. Our study of church unity has brought out many symbolic functions of ecumenicity. In many church circles it is associated with high status and serves to confer prestige upon those who participate in the movement. Often laymen and clergymen deem it a special honor to attend church unity conferences and meetings as delegates. Its symbolic function is also evidenced in the community-church label in order to remove the stigma of foreignness or lower-class derivation associated with some denominations. The symbol of religious unity to the outside world is expressed vividly in ecumenical sponsorship of religious observances.

9. The emergence of rational ecumenical institutions is not merely a passive response to external social circumstances; in many instances it signifies a reaction against cultural exigencies for the sake of grappling with negative features in the social order. Examples of this response earlier examined are the founding of the Federal Council of Churches, organic mergers which bridge apparent social differences, the Council of Community Churches, and local community-centered churches, such as the East Harlem Protestant Parish. The unitive response to overcome social differences and to make an effective impact upon the non-Christian world, is a recurrent theme in the drive toward church unity. It suggests an incentive which issues partly from the wellsprings of reaction against culture rather than a drift with it. The ambiguous role of the churches and the claim it is not entirely adaptive in its interaction with culture is thereby substantiated.[1]

These propositions serve to highlight some of the many social sources of church unity amplified in preceding chapters.

---

[1] For a perceptive analysis of the relationship between the Church and culture cf. H. Richard Niebuhr, *Christ and Culture* (New York: Harper & Brothers, 1953).

221

There remains only to add a few concluding postscripts. Therefore, some tantalizating problems and queries which were confronted along the way, but were either tangential to the main theme or emerged as implications or unresolved issues, will now be voiced. Perhaps these issues should be best framed as questions that point the path for both the reader and the writer to ponder further, before rushing in to fill the void with rational explanations.

1. Does the correlation of church unity and cultural unity mean that the church simply cooperates with the real tendency of the world? Or, is there an autonomous function of the Church in the world which has not been justly treated?

2. Although our focus has been almost exclusively on the way the church unity movement reflects the growing unity of American society, is it not possible that cultural unity reflects, in some measure, the unity of the Church, particularly in the latter's precepts, if not in its institutions? What impact does church unity have on social unity, or social differences?

3. What is the significance of the development of consensus in American Protestantism? Is there any validity to the charge that such developments are ushering in a new kind of institutional rigidity? In the long run, what will such tendencies imply for voluntarism—the great tradition of the American churches?

4. With the development of new rational structures of ecumenicity, is there sufficient clarity about the lodging of authority? If the problem of authority remains ambiguous, will the result be responsibility without power?

5. Does organic merger between denominations necessarily result in the development of new splinter groups? Are the new schisms which accompany many church unions relatively inconsequential? What role does the possibility of new schisms play in the deterrence of church union?

6. Why is it that a group like the Disciples of Christ, which was founded on the impulse of Christian unity, has been involved in so many discussions about church unity, but is never able to consummate a union?

7. What are the legitimate institutional forms and expressions of church unity? Is there not a clear danger that if ecumenicity remains an idea—and ideal—it will fail for lack of communication? Is there not an equal danger that if it finds expression in particular institutional forms, it will become ossified and fall short of its originating impetus?

These, then, are some of the questions which have loomed from time to time, and will continue to plague the writer; some of these unanswered questions suggest new directions of research.

Finally, it should be pointed out that our chapter on "Countervailing Movements" yielded unanticipated consequences. In analyzing the resurgence of denominationalism, the rise of sectarianism and fundamentalism, and the Southern Baptist Convention, we discovered that fewer concessions and qualifications of the theory of social sources of church unity were necessary than had been anticipated. In the main, these "negative cases" tended more to affirm than to deny the validity of our interpretation.

It is our fondest hope that the preliminary findings embodied in this exploratory study might stimulate others to further research and progressive revision or modification of the suggestions, observations, and hypotheses advanced in these pages; and that the fruitfulness and potentialities of such investigation have, in some measure, been demonstrated.

I have portrayed the church unity movement as a part of the drama of cultural transformation, particularly as that drama has been unfolding over the past three decades. The interaction of church and society has been guided by the thought that dynamic changes in a society are capable of playing a role that draws together diverse groups, just as they can provide the occasion for splitting groups apart. The thrusts of social change are not unidirectional. There are no inexorable laws which preordain that social factors must operate solely as centrifugally divisive forces. If, as has been suggested, the diversity of religious bodies in America reflects the spirit of free enterprise in a business society,[2] then quite possibly, the unity of religious groups reflects the merging and nucleation in business, and the increasing control which checks an unbridled free enterprise system.

Our time is a moment in history in which religious forces have converged with social factors, such as race, class, sectionalism, nationalism, and the various patterns of unity, to produce a very imposing movement of church unity. It is a period which has witnessed an alternation from disunity to increasing unity among Protestant groups. How is man to explain such great turnings of the tide, which is surely not yet taken at its flood? The social sources of church unity is offered as a partial interpretation. At the end of the day, however, when man's reckoning has ground to a halt, we are left facing the sheer givenness of the fact of the dawning of the church unity movement in American Protestantism.

[2] Yinger, *op. cit.*, p. 293.

SELECTED
BIBLIOGRAPHY

Angell, Robert C. *The Integration of American Society*. New York: Mc-Graw-Hill Book Company, 1941.

——. *Free Society and Moral Crisis*. Ann Arbor: University of Michigan Press, 1958.

Baron, Salo W. *Modern Nationalism and Religion*. New York: Harper & Brothers, 1947.

Bass, Archer. *Protestantism in the United States*. New York: Thomas Y. Crowell Company, 1929.

Beach, Waldo. "Euphoria in Suburbia," *Christianity and Crisis* (April 2, 1956).

Bennett, John C. "The Forms of Ecumenical Christianity," *Toward World Wide Christianity*, ed. O. F. Nolde. New York: Harper & Brothers, 1946.

——. "The Responsible Society," *Social Action* (November 1954.)

Bilheimer, Robert S. *The Quest for Christian Unity*. New York: Association Press, 1952.

Bonderud, Omar, and Lutz, Charles (Eds.). *America's Lutherans*. Columbus, Ohio: Wartburg Press, 1955.

Boulding, Kenneth. *The Organizational Revolution*. New York: Harper & Brothers, 1953.

Bradshaw, Marion J. *Baleful Legacy*. Oklahoma City: Modern Publishers, Inc., 1955.

Brauer, Jerald C. *Protestantism in America*. Philadelphia: The Westminster Press, 1953.

Brown, William Adams. *Toward a United Church*. New York: Charles Scribner's Sons, 1946.

Brunner, Edmund de S. *The Larger Parish*. New York: Institute of Social and Religious Research, 1934.

Burkhart, Roy. "The Community Church," *Christendom*, XI (Spring, 1946).

Cavert, Samuel McCrea. "Christian Unity in America," *The Church*

Through Half a Century, eds. Samuel McCrea Cavert and H. P. Van Dusen. New York: Charles Scribner's Sons, 1936.

———. "The Ecumenical Movement: Retrospect and Prospect," *Ecumenical Review* (April, 1958).

Committee on the War and the Religious Outlook *Christian Unity: Its Principles and Possibilities.* New York: Association Press, 1921.

Clark, E. T. "Non-Theological Factors in Religious Diversity," *Ecumenical Review* (July, 1951).

Craig, Clarence T. *The One Church in the Light of the New Testament.* Nashville: Abingdon Press, 1951.

Cuber, John, and Harper, Robert. *Problems of American Society: Values in Conflict.* New York: Henry Holt and Company, 1949.

De Tocqueville, Alexis. *Democracy in America.* New York: Vintage Books, Inc., 1954.

Dodd, C. H.; Cragg, G. R.; Ellul, Jacques. *Social and Cultural Factors in Church Divisions.* New York: World Council of Churches, 1952.

Dornbusch, S. M. and Irle, R. D. "The Failure of Presbyterian Union," *American Journal of Sociology,* LXIV (January 1959), 352-55.

Douglass, H. Paul. *Church Comity.* New York: Doubleday, Doran and Company, 1929.

———. *Church Unity Movements in the United States.* New York: Institute of Social and Religious Research, 1934.

———. *A Decade of Objective Progress in Church Unity, 1927-1936.* New York: Harper & Brothers, 1937.

———. "Cultural Differences and Recent Religious Divisions," *Christendom* (Winter, 1945), 89-105.

———. *The Comity Report.* New York: Commission on Planning and Adjustment of Local Inter-Church Relations, 1950.

———. "Ecumenicity in America," *Toward World Wide Christianity,* ed. O. F. Nolde. New York: Harper & Brothers, 1946.

———. *United Local Churches.* New York: Federal Council of Churches, n.d.

Duff, Edward, S. J. *The Social Thought of the World Council of Churches.* London: Longmans, Green and Company, 1956.

Dun, Angus. *The Meaning of Unity.* New York: Harper & Brothers, 1937.

———. *Prospecting for a United Church.* New York: Harper & Brothers, 1948.

Felton, Ralph A. *Local Church Cooperation in Rural Communities.* New York: Home Missions Council, n.d.

Fukuyama, Yoshio. *New Churches Aided by the Board of Home Missions, 1944-1955.* New York: Congregational Christian Churches, 1957.

———. "The Theological Implications of Mobility," *Christian Unity in North America,* ed. J. Robert Nelson. St. Louis: The Bethany Press, 1958.

Furniss, Norman F. *The Fundamentalist Controversy, 1918-1931.* New Haven: Yale University Press, 1954.

Garrison, Winfred E. "Social and Cultural Factors in our Divisions," *Ecumenical Review* (October, 1952), 43-51.

———. *Christian Unity and the Disciples of Christ.* St. Louis: The Bethany Press, 1955.

———. *The Quest and Character of a United Church.* Nashville: Abingdon Press, 1957.

Hallenbeck, Wilbur C. *The Minneapolis Churches and Their Comity Problems.* New York: Institute of Social and Religious Research, 1929.

Handlin, Oscar. *The Uprooted; the Epic Story of the Great Migrations That Made the American People.* Boston: Little, Brown and Company, 1951.

Handy, Robert T. *We Witness Together.* New York: Friendship Press, 1956.

Hodgson, Leonard. *The Ecumenical Movement.* Sewanee, Tenn.: University of the South Press, 1951.

Hooker, Elizabeth. *United Churches.* New York: George H. Doran, 1926.

———. *Religion in the Highlands.* New York: Home Missions Council, 1933.

Hopkins, C. Howard. *History of the YMCA in North America.* New York: Association Press, 1951.

Horton, Douglas, and Richards, George W. "The Spirit of a Proposed Union," *Christendom* (Summer, 1943).

Horton, Douglas. "Now the United Church of Christ," *Christian Century* (June 12, 1957).

Horton, Walter M. *Toward a Reborn Church.* New York: Harper & Brothers, 1953.

———. *Christian Theology: An Ecumenical Approach.* New York: Harper & Brothers, 1955.

Hudson, Winthrop. *The Great Tradition of the American Churches.* New York: Harper & Brothers, 1953.

Hutchison, John A. *We Are Not Divided.* New York: Round Table Press, 1941.

Jacob, Philip E. *Changing Values in College.* New Haven: Edward W. Hazen Foundation, 1956.

Jenkins, Daniel. "The Ecumenical Movement and Its Non-Theological Factors," *Ecumenical Review* (July, 1951).

Kallen, Horace. *Culture and Democracy in the United States.* New York: Boni and Liveright, 1924.

———. *Cultural Pluralism and the American Idea.* Philadelphia: University of Pennsylvania Press, 1956.

Kean, Charles D. *The Road to Reunion.* Greenwich, Conn: The Seabury Press, 1958.

Kik, J. Marcellus. *Ecumenism and the Evangelical.* Philadelphia: Presbyterian and Reformed Publishing Co., 1958.

Knox, John. *The Early Church and the Coming Great Church.* Nashville: Abingdon Press, 1955.

Lantz, J. Edward. "Church Councils in the South," *The Pastor* (August, 1956).

Lawrence, J. B. *Cooperating Southern Baptists*. Atlanta: Home Mission Board, Southern Baptist Convention, 1949.

Leinberger, Hugo. "The Church in the 'New Suburb,'" *Religious Education* (January-February, 1955).

Lee, Robert. *Protestant Churches in the Brooklyn Heights*. New York: Brooklyn Division of the Protestant Council, 1954.

———. "The Oberlin Conference," *Christianity and Crisis* (September 30, 1957).

Lee, Robert, and Roy, Ralph. "The Negro Church," *Christian Century* (October 30, 1957).

Leiper, Henry Smith. "Reunion and the Ecumenical Movement" *Protestant Thought in the Twentieth Century*, ed. Arnold S. Nash. New York: The Macmillan Company, 1951.

Lerner, Max. *America as a Civilization*. New York: Simon and Schuster, Inc., 1957.

Lipset, Seymour M., and Rogoff, Natalie. "Class and Opportunity in the United States and Europe," *Commentary* (December, 1954).

Loescher, Frank S. *The Protestant Church and the Negro*. New York: Association Press, 1948.

Macfarland, Charles S. *Church Unity in Practice and Prophecy*. New York: The Macmillan Company, 1933.

Mackay, John A. "The Ecumenical Goal," *Toward World Wide Christianity*, ed. O. F. Nolde. New York: Harper & Brothers, 1946.

McNeill, John T. "Protestantism," *Religion and Our Divided Denominations*, ed. Willard L. Sperry. Cambridge: Harvard University Press, 1945.

Mead, Frank S. *Handbook of Denominations in the United States*. Nashville: Abingdon Press, 1956.

Merton, Robert K. *Social Theory and Social Structure*. Chicago: Free Press of Glencoe, Ill., 1957.

Miller, Kenneth. "Our Growing Suburbs and Their Churches," *Religion in Life* (Autumn, 1955).

Minear, Paul. "Action and Reaction in Ecumenical Movement," *Religion in Life* (Spring, 1957).

———. (ed.) *The Nature of the Unity We Seek*. St. Louis: The Bethany Press, 1958.

Moore, John M. *The Long Road to Methodist Union*. Nashville: Abingdon Press, 1943.

Morrison, Charles C. *The Unfinished Reformation*. New York: Harper & Brothers, 1953.

Muelder, Walter G. "Institutionalism in Relation to Unity and Disunity," *The Nature of the Unity We Seek*, ed. Paul S. Minear. St. Louis: The Bethany Press, 1958.

———. *Foundations of the Responsible Society*. Nashville: Abingdon Press, 1959.

Murch, James Deforest. *Cooperation Without Compromise: A History of the National Association of Evangelicals.* Grand Rapids, Mich.: Wm. B. Eerdmans Publishing Company, 1956.

Neill, Stephen, and Rouse, Ruth. *A History of the Ecumenical Movement.* Philadelphia: The Westminster Press, 1954.

Newbigen, J. E. L. *The Reunion of the Church.* London, Student Christian Movement Press, 1948.

Niebuhr, Reinhold. "The Ecumenical Issue in the United States," *Theology Today* (January, 1946).

Niebuhr, H. Richard. *The Social Sources of Denominationalism.* New York: Henry Holt and Company, 1929.

————. *The Kingdom of God in America.* Chicago: Willett, Clark, and Company, 1937.

Nishi, S. F. "The Unity of the Church." Unpublished Ph.D. dissertation, Department of Religion, Columbia University, 1950.

Nottingham, Elizabeth K. *Religion and Society.* New York: Doubleday & Company, 1954.

Obendiek, H. "The Social and Cultural Factors in Church Division." London: Student Christian Movement Press, 1953.

Outler, Albert. *The Christian Tradition and the Unity We Seek.* New York: Oxford University Press, 1957.

Oxnam, G. Bromley. *On This Rock.* New York: Harper & Brothers, 1951.

Piper, David R. *Community Churches.* Chicago: Willett, Clark and Colby, 1928.

Pope, Liston. *Millhands and Preachers.* New Haven: Yale University Press, 1942.

Price, Theron D. "A Southern Baptist Views Church Unity," *Church Unity in North America,* ed. J. Robert Nelson. St. Louis: The Bethany Press, 1958.

Riesman, David; Glazer, Nathan; Denney, Reul. *The Lonely Crowd.* New Haven: Yale University Press, 1950.

Rice, Clayton S. "United Protestant Churches," *The City Church* (January-February, 1954), pp. 27-30.

Rosenberg, Bernard, and White, David M. (eds.). *Mass Culture.* Chicago: The Free Press of Glencoe, Ill., 1957.

Sanderson, Ross. *The Strategy of City Church Planning.* New York: Harper & Brothers, 1932.

————. "Toward a More Ecumenical Church." Lake Geneva: Association of Council Secretaries, 1943.

————. *The Church Serves the Changing City.* New York: Harper & Brothers, 1955.

Sanford, E. (ed.). *The Federal Council of Churches of Christ in America.* Westwood, N. J.: Fleming H. Revell Company.

Sangrey, Abram. "A Younger Church in America: The United Church, Los Alamos, New Mexico," *Ecumenical Review,* III (October, 1950), 29-41.

Schneider, Herbert W. *Religion in Twentieth Century America.* Cambridge: Harvard University Press, 1952.

Shedd, Clarence P. *Two Centuries of Student Christian Movements.* New York: Association Press, 1934.

Silcox, Claris E. *Church Union in Canada.* New York: Institute of Social and Religious Research, 1933.

Sklare, Marshall. *Conservative Judaism.* Chicago: The Free Press of Glencoe, Ill., 1955.

Slosser, Gaius Jackson. *Christian Unity.* New York: E. P. Dutton & Company, 1929.

Sperry, Willard. "The Non-Theological Factors in the Making and Unmaking of Church Union." Geneva: Faith and Order Paper, No. 84, 1937.

Sweet, William Warren. *Religion on the American Frontier.* 4 vols. Chicago: University of Chicago Press, 1931, 1936, 1939, 1946.

――――. *American Culture and Religion.* Dallas: Southern Methodist University Press, 1951.

Tigner, Hugh S. "Localizing the Ecumenical," *Christian Century* (April 6, 1955).

Tulga, Chester E. *The Case Against the Federal Council of Churches.* Chicago: Conservative Baptist Fellowship, n.d.

Turner, Frederick Jackson. *The Significance of the Frontier in American History.* Proceedings of the State Historical Society of Wisconsin, 1893.

Underwood, Kenneth. *Protestant and Catholic.* Boston: Beacon Press, 1957.

Van Dusen, Henry P. "The Issues of Christian Unity," *Christendom,* XI (Spring, 1946), 327-40.

――――. *World Christianity.* New York: Abingdon-Cokesbury Press, 1947.

――――. "Councils in Crisis," *Theology Today,* IX (January, 1953).

Vidich, Arthur J., and Bensman, Joseph. *Small Town in Mass Society.* Princeton: Princeton University Press, 1958.

Visser 't Hooft, W. A. "The Word 'Ecumenical,' " *A History of the Ecumenical Movement,* eds. Stephen Neill and Ruth Rouse. Philadelphia: The Westminster Press, 1954.

Wach, Joachim. *Types of Religious Experience.* Chicago: University of Chicago Press, 1951.

Warner, W. Lloyd and Lunt, Paul. *The Social Life of a Modern Community.* New Haven: Yale University Press, 1941.

――――. *American Life: Dream and Reality.* Chicago: University of Chicago Press, 1953.

Warren, W. J., and Powers, R. L. "A Study of Denominational Changes Made by Students at Yale Divinity School." New Haven: Social Ethics Library, 1954.

Wedel, T. O. *The Coming Great Church.* New York: The Macmillan Company, 1945.

Weigel, Gustav, S. J. "American Roman Catholicism and Ecumenism," *Lutheran World,* V (June, 1958).

Whyte, William H. *The Organization Man.* New York: Simon and Schuster, Inc., 1956.

Williams, Colin. "Theological Backgrounds of the Ecumenical Movement." Unpublished Ph.D. dissertation, Drew University, School of Theology, 1957.

Williams, Robin M. *American Society.* New York: Alfred A. Knopf, Inc., 1951.

World Council of Churches. *The Christian Hope and the Task of the Church.* New York: Harper & Brothers, 1954.

Yinger, J. Milton. *Religion, Society and the Individual: An Introduction to the Sociology of Religion.* New York: The Macmillan Company. 1957.

Yinger, J. Milton, and Simpson, G. "Can Segregation Survive in an Industrial Society?" *The Antioch Review,* XVIII (March, 1958).

Zangwill, Israel. *The Melting Pot.* New York: The Macmillan Company, 1923.

INDEX

233

235